The Handbook of
VINTAGE CIGARETTE
Lighters

STUART SCHNEIDER
& IRA PILOSSOF

Schiffer Publishing Ltd

4880 Lower Valley Road, Atglen, PA 19310 USA

Designed by Bonnie M. Hensley
Layout by Tammy Ward & Becky Riggins
Type set in Bodoni Bk BT/Aldine721 BT

ISBN: 0-7643-0932-3
Printed in China
1 2 3 4

Published by Schiffer Publishing Ltd.
4880 Lower Valley Road
Atglen, PA 19310
Phone: (610) 593-1777; Fax: (610) 593-2002
E-mail: Schifferbk@aol.com
Please visit our web site catalog at
www.schifferbooks.com

In Europe, Schiffer books are distributed by
Bushwood Books
6 Marksbury Avenue Kew Gardens
Surrey TW9 4JF England
Phone: 44 (0)181 392-8585;
Fax: 44 (0)181 392-9876
E-mail: Bushwd@aol.com

This book may be purchased from the publisher.
Include $3.95 for shipping. Please try your bookstore first.
We are interested in hearing from authors with book ideas on related subjects.
You may write for a free printed catalog.

ONTENTS

We have strove for only quality photographs for our book. This book will hopefully stand out among the others with its crisp, clear photography. Our publisher has gone the extra mile to reproduce the quality of the photographs so that you can actually see close-up what we saw. We have attempted to give as much information as possible and show you a wide array of lighters. With regards to the pricing, it was extremely important to us that it be done as accurately and as fairly as possible with a range of values, rather than simply one price. Of course there are many times when a collector will pay almost anything to acquire a certain piece for his or her collection. We have based the values on our observations and knowledge, and on our discussions with other collectors when more input was needed. We also consulted a long-time friend and fellow collector, Guy Nishida, on every lighter photographed so as to get a coast-to-coast feel of reasonable prices.

ACKNOWLEDGMENTS

The authors would like to acknowledge the many individuals who lent valuable assistance in the creation of this book. By permitting us to view and photograph their collections, we can now share their lighters with the rest of the world. We thank Bruce Huberman for the majority of the Ronson pieces pictured herein, as well as his time and enthusiasm and Bob Brockmann for the use of his Zippos and his expertise; Tom Clarke, Jon Costanza, Linda Meabon of the Zippo Company, and Paul Gifford for their valued input; Paul Schofield for lending us his miniature lighter jewelry collection; and Judith Sanders, founder of "On The Lighter Side," the international lighter collector's club—no one has done more to promote the growth and respectability of the hobby than Ms. Sanders.

We especially wish to acknowledge the contributions of Larry Tolkin. Larry is a long-time collector possessing an awe-inspiring collection as well as a wealth of lighter knowledge.

Last, but not least, we wish to thank Guy Nishida, good friend and well-known lighter expert. His expertise on Scriptos was particularly helpful. He combed through all of our work providing comments as well as a West Coast valuation perspective. We believe that our book is more accurate and unbiased as a result.

Once again, our thanks to all of these individuals for their time, their marvelous lighters, and above all their willingness to share so much of their knowledge with us.

iv

FOREWORD

When first asked by Stuart Schneider to co-author a book on lighters, I was elated and agreed to it instantly. I had worked with Stuart on his first lighter book, *Cigarette Lighters*, and the experience was wonderful. I felt my eighteen years of passionate lighter collecting certainly qualified me for the task that lay ahead. I was prepared and excited to write about a subject I had come to know very well. Since many of the more unusual and beautiful lighters do not show up often at specialized shows any more, it required some work (and finesse) to find great lighters. My goal was to share what I had learned, by locating and photographing some of the finest and most interesting cigarette lighters to include in our book. In this way we could give new collectors an opportunity to appreciate these "works of art" designed solely for the purpose of lighting one's cigarette. Being lucky enough to have begun collecting years before the current interest in lighters, I have been able to observe the hobby and its growth from its infancy.

It is with this background that I joined Stuart to create a book that would be informative, accurate, and interesting.

Ira Pilossof

INTRODUCTION

We felt that there was a current need to have a new reference book with lots of lighters and loads of photographs. When collectors are out on the chase, they need a quick reference to see what they have, what is available, and the values of lighters new to them. This book is arranged in an effort to provide collectors with easily accessible information. Over 800 lighters are illustrated in full color. They are shown in alphabetical order, by company name, and by date within each company listing. The available historical data is presented clearly and concisely. When a cigarette lighter's brand name was unavailable or secondary, we listed the lighter under "Unknown," "Trench Art," "Occupied Japan," "Chemical," and such. We have tried to make it easy for you to find the lighter that you are holding in your hand.

This book includes a large variety of lighters with most being wick or petrol models, dating from the 1880s to the 1950s. Without producing an encyclopedia, the attempt has been to broaden the number of lighters illustrated. In an effort to appeal to new collectors, who many times start out collecting from well-known companies, makers such as Dunhill, Ronson, Evans, Scripto, and Zippo are included. Also, many longtime collectors have established collections by these makers. In addition to the more familiar names, the book also includes unusual and interesting lighters from smaller companies. We have included a nice selection of each. If you can not find your lighter in this book, you may want to check out *Cigarette Lighters*, by Schneider & Fischler. The reasons a lighter may not appear are that it may be extremely rare, extremely common, unavailable (to us at the time), or similar to another that is illustrated.

We realize there are many collectors of the newer lighters of today, such as Marlboro and Camel, and also Zippo collectors who collect each new edition produced. We have tried to show a few examples of these but, for the most part, have concentrated on vintage lighters. Their collectiblity has increased tremendously over the past five years. It appears that their appeal is due to a number of reasons, beginning with their beauty.

The artist designed lighters, especially the Art Deco models, are more than simply a way to light a cigarette. Many were enameled much the same as fine jewelry. They capture and reflect the feeling of the 1930s.

The Art Deco movement started in France in the mid 1920s. It began with the geometric shapes that echoed the designs of the buildings in modern cities. Soon these stepped lines were streamlined and given rounded edges. Cigarette lighter designers moved their designs onto the popular lighters of the day, creating art that you could carry in your pocket. Competition is stiff in the field of Art Deco collecting. Design collectors want everything with these modern patterns. They have discovered that since cigarette lighters are small, beautiful, and on the whole relatively inexpensive, they are the perfect item to collect.

Around the time of the Great Depression the average worker could not afford to buy an expensive artist designed lighter. Manufacturers of inexpensive lighters picked up on the demand for lighters and hundreds were made with modern artistic designs. Ronson jumped into the Art Deco design craze with both feet, making hundreds of designs during the 1930s. The section on Ronson lighters has been expanded to show dozens of these exceptionally beautiful lighters and combination lighter/cigarette cases.

The small size of lighters has positively impacted their popularity. Some people call them pocket collectibles. A nice collection can be displayed in a small area and they travel well when visiting other lighter collectors or lighter shows. Try that with collectible tractor seats!

Cigarette lighter collecting has continued to grow in a steady and organized manner. We start out mentioning this because collecting fields that grow steadily and in an orderly fashion tend to survive and attract new collectors. We have also found that popular collecting subjects generate a continuing stream of new and useful books. With the growing litigation and governmental restrictions on smoking, cigarette lighter collecting seems destined to be a popular hobby long after there are no more cigarettes to light. It supports two major United States lighter collector clubs as well as active groups in Asia, Great Britain, and other parts of Europe.

Collecting is fun and collections should be exciting. Lighters such as Dunhill, Ronson, and Zippo are becoming harder to find and are often priced "by the book." This usually means that few bargains are available. Dealers and collectors are knowledgeable about these lighter values and their appeal. This book also includes many interesting, extremely well-made, but less well-known, lighters, whose appeal is only just beginning to be recognized. Since the book *Cigarette Lighters* came out, the market for Scripto lighters has burgeoned. New collectors and seasoned collectors alike are buying every Scripto that they can find. Will you be able to recognize this hot collectible of the 21st century? Once you have seen an example in this book, you will be more likely to recognize one when you are out hunting for lighters.

Lighter clubs and lighter shows have been attracting larger and larger numbers of people. Access to the Internet has opened up a whole new world of collecting. If you have not yet heard about eBay, the on-line auction service, you should check it out (see resources at the end of the book). Hundreds of lighters are being auctioned every day on **eBay**. Now collectors from around the world are competing with collectors throughout the United States for great lighters.

There are many benefits to auctions. They are able to offer pieces that would otherwise be unavailable elsewhere. A great lighter, sitting in a little antique shop, in a rural area where towns are 50 miles apart, may never sell, if the right collector fails to come along. If that same lighter is put on auction on the Internet, thousands of collectors will see it and bid it up to market value. Competitive bidding brings out the good items. New collectors are entering the field and some people are buying for investment rather than in order to add items to their collection. The seemingly expensive lighter you pass up today will be the one you remember tomorrow.

ABOUT PRICING

Valuing lighters is complex in this quickly escalating collecting field. It has been said that price guides are out of date by the time they are published. We have worked with many collectors and dealers to set price ranges. Pricing is part science, part art, and part crystal ball gazing. A popular book on Beanie Babies predicts the value of the little critters 10 years in the future. We look for market trends and collector interest then try to predict the values for a few years in the future. Time will show this guide to be accurate. We think we have it right when half the people say the prices are too high and the other half say they are too low. Collectors need to feel assured of what they are spending and not feel as if they are being overcharged. There are auctions, mail order dealers, antique dealers, private collectors, and other places where pieces may be purchased. The same lighter may sell for $15.00 at a flea market and be offered for $150.00 at an antique store in a city. Which price is correct? Since some of the pieces are unique and demand varies by region, prices for one piece may not reflect prices for a similar item. Prices on good items (of good quality and in good condition) have at least doubled over the last few years.

Values are given in ranges and we have tried to assign values at which dealers can sell and collectors will buy. The dealers have not set "top dollar" prices and the buyers are not paying "through the nose." It is believed that these ranges reflect fair prices at which lighters will usually trade. The person that you deal with may or may not follow these "rules." **Note: All lighters are valued in excellent condition**, regardless of the condition of the item in the photograph, unless otherwise noted in the value. If the item is not *excellent*, it is worth less. If it is *mint* or *mint in the box*, it is often worth more.

As high as prices may seem, money alone can not put together a good collection. Some pieces may be one of only a few known and the collectors who own those pieces may want to hold on to them. They are often not for sale at any price. Even if you have thousands to spend, it may take you lots of time, effort, and/or personal contacts to buy a piece when it comes on the market.

WHY THE LIGHTER WAS INVENTED

Early man found that fire was essential to life. It kept him warm, cooked his food, and enabled him to see in the dark. Eventually, man learned to use fire to forge tools. The earliest mechanical methods for making fire were striking flint, a hard and glassy looking rock, on iron or steel. This produced a shower of sparks that could start a fire in dry kindling. The beauty of flint and steel was that it was easily transportable and virtually water resistant.

However, with the introduction of firearms in warfare, a more consistent method of creating fire became necessary. Early guns used a smoldering rope to ignite the powder, a method that could be considered the first easily portable lighter. (Legend has it that Blackbeard, the famous pirate, went into battle with smoldering ropes stuck in his hat. If one rope was extinguished, another burning rope was available to fire his guns. I guess that this is where the term "beard burn" originated.)

The idea of a smoldering rope was not everyone's idea of a great portable lighter. In the 1840s, wooden matches became popular. These were cheap and reliable. People who smoked pipes and cigars generally lit these matches or wooden sticks by dipping them into the flame of a candle, fireplace, or lantern.

In the 1860s, petroleum oils began to replace and supplement whale oil. Oil drilling and refining became a money-making business. The cigarette though invented in the mid-1850s did not become popular until the 1880s. During the late 1870s and early 1880s, cigarette making machines were invented as a way to allow the southern tobacco farmers and marketers to sell more tobacco. It was during this time also that interest in a cigarette lighter began to spread.

Man, as inventor, was constantly looking for ways to improve upon objects of daily use. Dozens of patents were filed for fire starter devices. One early cigarette lighter was simply a smoldering cord that was lit with flint and steel, the same mechanism originally used on the matchlock rifles. Another device used was the Maynard tape primer, used on the Maynard rifle. It was sort of a cap gun that used fulminate of mercury caps to create a spark. This idea was transferred to the cigar lighter about 1877. The sparking cap caused a rope to smolder. Flint and steel were tried in many forms, but the early attempts usually wore out quickly or broke with daily use.

One novel idea adapted a chemical battery to create a spark or a heated coil to light a smoldering rope. In no time, inventors discovered that a bit of refined oil or gasoline made the rope burst into flame rather than smolder. Once the problems with flint and steel were resolved, the striker lighter became popular. It was simple. A piece of steel surrounded by a wick saturated in a refined oil was struck on a flint-bearing strip. It was only a matter of time before inventors would create a simple and reliable way to contain and improve the lighter. Again, the needs of war, in this case the first World War, pushed the technology forward to create a working lighter with a flint and wheel mechanism—and the modern lighter was born.

ABDULLA, c.1933. A French made chrome plated lighter with a body wrap that resembles enamel but is a form of plastic. Abdulla made pipes, lighters, and cigarettes during the 1920s to 1940s in France. They are extremely high quality lighters that used a unique mechanism. The company was purchased by the Querica family in the 1920s. Value: $125-175.

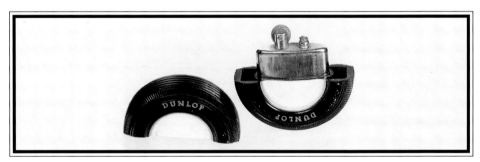

Advertiser, c.1950. A figural tire shaped lighter advertising Dunlop Tires. The two halves pull apart to show the simple wick and wheel type lighter. Value: $100-125.

Advertisers, 1950s. A group of Japanese flat, advertising lighters. With advertising lighters, the value follows the Zippo rule (see what is more valuable in Zippo advertising lighters in the Zippo section). These were very popular in the 1950s and 1960s. Value: $20-50.

Advertisers, c.1958. A group of advertising lighters made in Japan. The center lighter is also musical with the winding mechanism on the back side. When the lighter is pushed, the music plays. 2" to 3" tall. Value: (L-R) $35-65, $85-150, $35-65.

Advertisers, c.1960. Three lighters with advertising on the sides. These are called "flat advertisers" by collectors and they were made in Japan. There are many variations and value depends on the company advertising and the design. Value: $15-35.

ALAIR, c.1930. The Alair was made in France and distinguishes itself by its great windscreen design. It is covered in red leather. Value: $150-200.

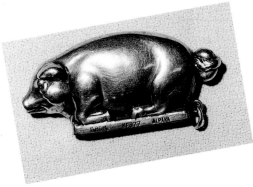

ALPACA, c.1915. A wonderful silver pig shaped striker lighter. 2.5" long. Value: $200-300.

ALPACA, c.1922. A German made striker lighter in silver plate. The shape is a soccer ball. Value: $150-200.

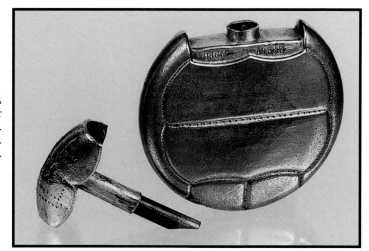

AMBASSADOR, c.1935. Three Ambassador lift arm lighters with various finishes. 2.5" tall. Value: $35-60.

AMERICAN, c.1940. A U.S. made lighter with a plastic type of material for the outer shell. Value: $150-200.

APOLLO STUDIOS, c.1935. A pitcher shaped lighter in a gold plated metal. The shape is similar to an Evans. 5" tall. Value: $150-200.

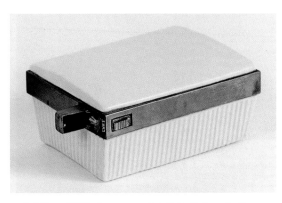

A.S.R., c.1945. An unusual A.S.R. lighter built into the side of a porcelain cigarette box. 3" tall. Value: $70-95.

A.S.R., c.1948. American Safety Razor of Brooklyn, New York, made the A.S.R. chrome plated lighter. 3.5" tall. Value: $25-45.

AURORA, c.1959. A paper covered combination flashlight/lighter made in Japan. It used 2 "N" cells to make the light work. It can be found in 2 sizes. 2.5" tall. Value: $15-20.

AUSTRIAN, c.1935. An Art Deco green enamel on chrome "Pipe Lighter" with a German patent. For use, the lighter is held sideways; the flame comes out the gap on the left side. 2.75" tall. Value: $150-200.

AUTO GIANT, c.1953. A chrome plated Japanese lighter with a windscreen. 4" tall. Value: $35-55.

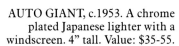

AUTO-LIGHT, c.1930. What a wonderful shape this French made lighter has. The high plunger projection was sure to snag every time it was withdrawn from the pocket. Chrome plated metal. Value: $100-150.

AUERMETAL, c.1925. An Austrian glass and chrome striker lighter. 4.75" tall. Value: $200-250.

AWR, c.1944. A handsome 9kt gold, English made lighter with engine turned design. A flick of the wheel exposes the wick and creates the spark. Value: $400-500.

BACH, c.1943. A handsome 9kt gold, English made lighter with engine turned design. Value: $500-600.

15

BAIER, c.1947. This German lighter, cigarette box, and ashtray was made of machined aluminum. Beautifully designed and functional, the handle on the door turns to activate the lighter and the top of the jeep opens to hold cigarettes. Nice touches include real rubber tires and even a spare tire. Baiers were made in Germany during the 1930s and 1940s and were generally made of aluminum. The post-war pieces are often marked "U.S. Zone." It is a high quality lighter that has an automatic-type mechanism. 14" long. Value: $150-250.

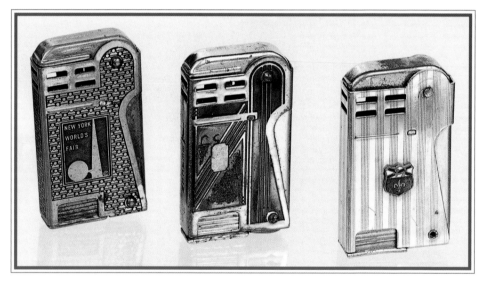

BEACON, c.1934. To operate the Beacon, you squeeze the sides, causing the top to open. It is similar to the U.S. made Regens lighter. Value: $150-175 (w/New York World's Fair imprint), $50-75 (standard designs).

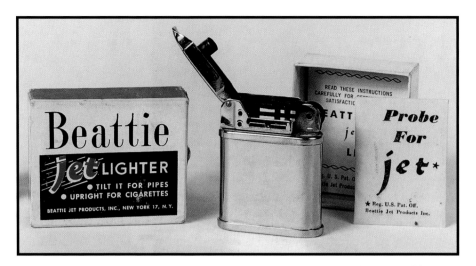

BEATTIE JET, c.1946. The Beattie Jet was a great lighter. It acted like a small blow torch when the lighter was tilted and the jet pipe was heated. The box claimed that it could do small soldering jobs and thaw frozen car locks. It was made in New York, but every pipe smoking New England college professor had to have one. A high quality pipe lighter (1945 to 1960s) available with different coverings in leather, sterling silver, etc. Value: $20 (without box), $60 (mint in the box w/instructions).

BENEY, c.1930 A wonderful lighter fluid dispenser in silver plated metal. Made in England and about 4" tall. Value: $150-200.

17

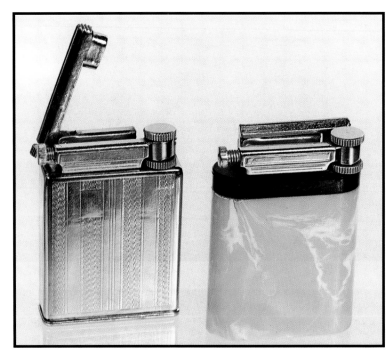

BENEY, c.1935. The Beney lighter, which was made in England, had an interesting double thumb wheel. Chrome plated metal and Bakelite. Bakelite, unlike regular plastic, was a fire resistant material. Value: $100-150.

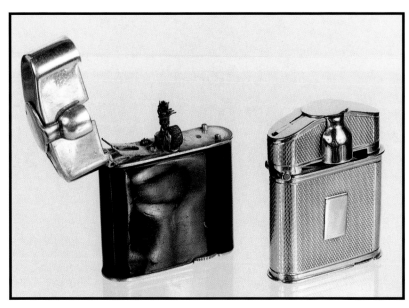

BENEY, c.1935. A pair of Beney lighters. The one on the left is slightly larger and is Sterling silver with black enamel. The one on the right is a smaller size in 9kt gold. Notice the unusual placement of the flint wheel. 2.5" and 2.75" tall. Value: (L-R) $500-700, $1,000-1,200.

BENLOW, c.1940. An interesting mechanism—when you turn the flint wheel, the lighter opens and lights. Chrome plate with an engine turned finish. Value: $100-125.

BLITZ, c.1938. A German made lighter. Silver plate with an engine turned finish. Value: $75-125.

BOWERS, c.1952. A great "Storm Master" lighter was given out by Lyndon Johnson when he was the Majority Leader in the Senate. Value: $50-75(when marked LBJ), $15-20 (plain).

BROWN & BIGELOW, c.1955. A box of "Colortone Windmaster" lighters used to show customers how their advertising will look on Brown & Bigelow lighters. The box contains six lighter inserts with lids that were interchangeable with the decorated base. Value: $100-130.

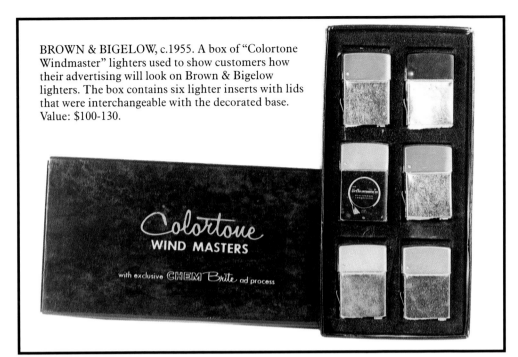

CAPITOL, c.1912. The Capitol is what a gadget-minded smoker would love to have on his or her desk. The intricate mechanism of springs and levers raises the snuffer cap, turns the flint wheel, and lights the lighter. These were produced in several sizes and finishes and were the only lighters that Capitol produced. Steele & Johnson Mfg., the maker of Capitol, was located in Waterbury, CT. This model incorporates an ashtray. Value: $100-150.

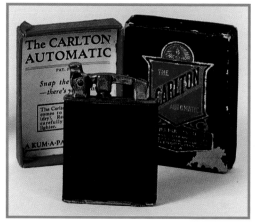

CARLTON, c.1923. Simple but sturdy, this thin Carlton automatic pocket lighter has a leather cover. Shown with its original box. The Carlton (1918 to 1930s) was a division of the Kum-a-part Company which made snap buttons for clothing. The mechanisms were high quality and the enamel overlay models are very desirable. All are very collectible. The company died with the Depression. Value: $75-125.

CARTIER, c.1926. A very elegant two-piece set—lighter and cigarette case—in Sterling silver and black enamel. Cartier (1847 to Present) was founded in Paris, France, by Louis Francois Cartier (1819-1904) who took over the shop of a jeweler named Picard. His work was of the highest caliber and he soon began to do work for King Louis Philippe and other royal and aristocrat families. His son, Alfred (1841-1925), joined him in 1872 and continued the tradition of high quality products. The firm moved to the Rue de la Paix in Paris in 1898. Alfred's son, Louis-Joseph, took over for his father around the turn of the century and began the detailed record keeping that is envied today. If you bought a Cartier product in 1900, Cartier had the records to show who made the product, when it was made, what it sold for, and when and to whom it was sold. The firm was innovative. For example, the wristwatch was an invention of Louis-Joseph. Lighter production was established after World War I. Lighters were produced before the war on an a per customer basis. Cartier produced wonderful lighters in precious metals with some containing precious gemstones. The demand increased for their lighters during the 1920s, and, by the late 1920s, their products were popular with customers other than the wealthy. They used high quality production methods and their products are well made and well conceived. Cartier introduced a gas model in 1968 called the Ovale. Value: $2,500-3,500 (w/case).

CARTIER, c.1933. A sterling silver Cartier cigarette lighter and dispenser. This is a fantastic flint and wick lighter which actually drops and lights one cigarette at a time. The lighting mechanism involves the use of a bladder in the lower part of the case that draws air through the cigarette, causing the flame to light the cigarette, as if someone inhaled as their cigarette was being lit. Value: $4,000-5,000.

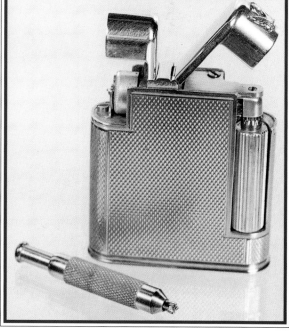

CARTIER, c.1941. A petrol lighter in Sterling silver. It has a nice ribbed design. Value: $400-500.

CARTIER, c.1940. A superb pencil/watch/lighter combination in Sterling silver. 5" long. Value: $1500-2300.

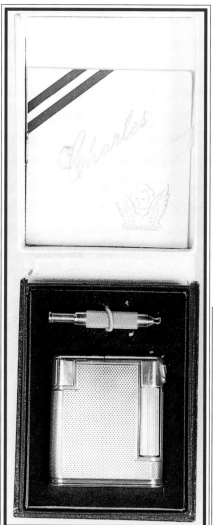

CHARLES, c.1949. A beautifully designed lighter with an unusual revolving flint chamber. The chamber revolved clockwise with each use so that the flint would wear evenly. The small tool was for adjusting the wick. Silver plated brass. Value: $500-600

CHASE & BRIAN, c.1954 & 1963. Two similar automatic American made lighters. Push the button to raise the snuffer and produce a flame. The one on the left is made by Chase Metal Products and the right one is marked "Brian." 3" tall. Value: (L-R) $25-50, $20-35.

Above & opposite page, bottom: Chemical, 1890. A wonderful French Potassium Bichromate lighter held by Rebecca. These early chemical lighters worked by combining zinc and carbon which produced an electrical charge that would ignite the fuel soaked wick affixed to the smaller bottle. Stands about 10" tall. Value: $600-800.

CHESTERFIELD, c.1925. The Chesterfield lighter is unusual in its shape. 2.5" tall. Value: $75-125.

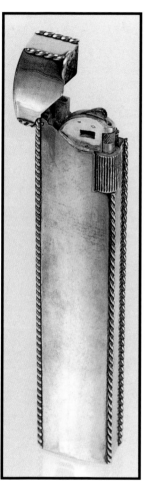

CHRISTIAN DIOR, c.1955 A Sterling silver desk lighter that used petrol. About 5.5" tall. Value: $800-1,000.

CLARK, 1920s. An unusual shaped Clark lighter. Usually the Clark was made with 4 sides. This model tapers down at each end to give it only 2 sides or a cushion effect. Gold plated brass. The company (1920s to 1940s) was located in North Attleborough, Mass., and made a nice solid, high quality lighter available in many styles including gold, silver, with watches, etc. Currently there is a high demand for these lighters. Value: $75-175.

CLARK, 1920s. A nice lift arm Clark lighter with a windguard in an ostrich leather covering. Value: $75-150.

CLARK, 1920s. A lift arm Clark lighter. Leather covered 18kt gold electroplate. Value: $40-80.

CLARK, c.1926. A five-sided gold plated lighter. This lighter has great Art Deco styling. 3" tall. A very desirable Clark lighter. Value: $350-400.

CLARK, c.1926. A very rare Japanese decorated Namiki lighter. The body is Sterling silver and both sides are shown. The maki-e lacquer work is highly sought by collectors. Usually one encounters models made by Dunhill and called Dunhill-Namiki. Value: $1,500-2,000.

CLARK, c.1928. An Art Deco Clark "Firefly" lighter in Sterling silver with enamel work. This is an exceptionally attractive lighter. 2.5" tall. Value: $500-700.

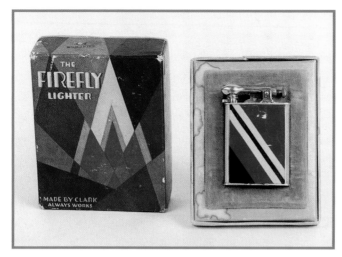

CLARK, c.1928. A very rare, in this condition, Clark "Firefly" lift arm lighter. This wonderful Art Deco lighter is lacquer painted. The paint is very prone to chipping. 3" tall. Value: $225-325 w/box.

CLODION, c.1940. A jerri-can shaped lighter that was made in France. The design is very true to an actual jerri-can. For example, the filler screw on the side resembles the real thing. Value: $100-175.

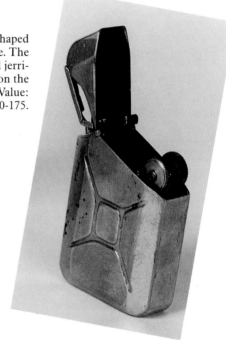

COLBY, c.1938. A beautiful Sterling silver pocket lighter made in Mt. Vernon, New York. When the top and bottom are pushed together, the center flower flap opens and the flame appears. This was produced by the Crosby Foundation established by Bing Crosby. 3" tall. Value: $200-275.

Collection. A nice selection of Ronson and Evans Art Deco combination lighter/cigarette cases. This is a strikingly beautiful assortment.

COLIBRI, c.1929. An "Original Kick Start", watch lighter in chrome plated metal. Colibri lighters were made from the 1920s. Originally it was a German firm called JBELO, which stood for Julius & Ben Lowenthal, that made pipes and lighters. In 1928, Julius developed the open spring mechanism on their "Original" model and Colibri introduced it. In 1933, the Colibri part moved to London, while JBELO stayed in Germany. It is a high quality lighter. Value: $1,200-1,400.

COLIBRI, c.1949. The Colibri metal flower when flipped over exposes the lighter. 2.5" tall. Usually marked "Occupied Germany." Value: $40-70.

COLIBRI, c.1952. A Colibri watch lighter (wick style). Gold plate over brass. Someone has inscribed this lighter with a 1966 date. Value: $150-200.

COLIBRI, c.1952. A Colibri watch lighter. Gold plate over brass. Value: $175-250.

COLIBRI, c.1952. A Toby jug wick model lighter. Long John Silver is ceramic with a brass insert. Part of a series of Royal Doulton lighter mugs. Value: $40-60.

COLIBRI, c.1980. The "Beam Sensor" was a very innovative lighter. This one, in brushed chrome, used a small electric eye to sense when your finger was placed in the slot, which caused the butane lighter to light. It is very hard, if not impossible, to repair and the battery is almost impossible to obtain; otherwise it is a very neat lighter. It originally sold for $125.00. Value: $75-125 (mint in the box).

CONSTELLATION, c.1938. A Bakelite plastic semi-automatic table lighter made in the United States. 3" tall. Value: $60-90.

D & O, c.1935. An automatic lighter with an unusual windscreen. 2.75" tall. Value: $125-175.

DANDY, c.1939. A French made lighter with a large double wheel. Chrome plate with engine turned finishes. Value: $75-100.

DIPLOMAT, c.1925. A Sport model lighter in chrome plated metal. 2.75" tall. Value: $100-150.

DOUGLASS, c.1926. A handsome table lighter of chrome plated brass. The design is engine turned and the mechanism is automatic. About 6" tall. Value: $250-300.

DOUGLASS, c.1926. A nickel plated brass lighter with a leather wrap. Value: $50-100.

DOME LIGHTER, c.1944. The Dome Lighter was distributed by Negbaur. As the name says, it is a dome shaped lighter. The bottom pulls out for refueling and the wick is on the top center, facing to the right rather than upward. Gold plated brass and black lacquer. Value: $60-90.

DOUGLASS, c.1926. The Douglass was a novel lighter. Douglas lighters were made in Menlo Park, California, and sometimes marked "Wrigley Bldg, Chicago." They made lighters for Van Cleef & Arpels and covered the market with

everything from inexpensive to elegant, expensive products. Their semi-automatic flying arm action is an eye catcher. A push of the lock button released the flying arm and caused a spark at the same time. This is a rare gold filled model with an engine turned design. Value: $500-600.

DOUGLASS TIFFANY, c.1926. A beautiful Sterling Silver Douglass lighter. This is a push button semi-automatic lighter that is marked "Douglass" and "Tiffany." Value: $350-550.

DUNHILL: 1907 to present

Dunhill was founded by Alfred Dunhill in 1907, and was located on Duke Street in London. Before 1907, Alfred ran a horse and carriage accessories shop founded by his father. With the advent of the automobile, the shop began to make quality items for the automobile driver. One successful item (1904) was a pipe with a built-in windscreen. Alfred left the automobile accessories business and began a pipe, tobacco, and smoking accessories shop. His first Alfred Dunhill pipe, made from the best briar, was introduced in 1910. The concept of the Dunhill shop was to offer the finest products. They cost more, but Dunhill did not want to compete with other tobacco shops on price, but on quality.

Dunhill's first lighter was the "Ednite," introduced in 1914. It was a pocket tinderwick lighter. The "Tinderwick," a pocket match style lighter, followed in 1916. With the advent of World War I, soldiers became the largest business segment for sales of pipes and tobacco. Dissatisfied with the lighters on the market, Alfred wanted to sell a lighter that was easy to use and could be lit with one hand. The "Every Time" lighter was introduced in the Christmas 1923-1924 catalog. It was made for Dunhill by the English company of Wise and Greenwood. Within a year, the "Every Time" became the "Unique." Demand was so high that the Geneva firm of La Nationale was hired to make the lighters. One of Dunhill's most famous styles, a lighter with a watch, was not a Dunhill idea but a customer's idea. Santiago Soulas, a wealthy South American customer, wanted a lighter with a watch in the side. Dunhill liked the idea and began making watch lighters in 1926.

In the 1922/1923 season, Dunhill created the Parker Pipe Company to sell pipes and smoking accessories that were not perfect enough to be called Dunhill. Parker Pipe was successful and it introduced a series of lighters sold under the name "Beacon."

The Namiki Manufacturing Company of Tokyo made a line of high quality products with hand painted finishes. They were looking for new markets and contacted Dunhill. Dunhill signed an exclusive agreement to sell the Dunhill-Namiki line of smoking accessories and writing intruments on July 8, 1930. On August 29, 1930, Dunhill signed an agreement with the American Safety Razor Company to market Dunhill lighters in America. Always looking to make his products better, an improved "Unique" model with a double wheel striker was introduced in 1931 along with a self-winding watch lighter. A minor problem for collectors is that many customers returned their single wheel lighters to Dunhill for updating to double wheel lighters. This makes the single wheel lighters rarer and could be confusing when dating an early double wheel lighter that has been modified by Dunhill.

The first (1933) Dunhill "Tallboy" lighter is unusual as it has both the Dunhill and Cartier names on it. Cartier held the patent, but Dunhill held the license to produce and sell it. Dunhill's Hunting Horn lighter was introduced in 1934. Its "Broadboy" line first appeared in 1936 along with a "Giant" model Unique lighter. 1938 saw the first Tinder Pistol Lighter and the Broadboy watch lighter came out in 1939.

Dunhill began working on a gas lighter in the late 1940s, and their first model, the "Rollagas," came out in 1956.

The Dunhill "Rollalite," a product exported only to Europe, came out in 1948. The "Sylph" first appeared in 1953, the same year as the "Aquarium." (Dunhill's records may not be accurate though, because the Aquarium is rumored to have appeared in a Christmas 1951 catalog.) The "Sylphide" came out in 1958, and the gas Sylphide model followed in 1965.

DUNHILL, 1920s. Unique model lift arm lighters. Production began in 1922 and each has a straight snuffer arm and a single wheel. The larger models are the B size, while the smaller is the A size Unique. Silver or gold plated, most were covered with fine leathers of ostrich or crocodile. Value: $75-125.

DUNHILL, c.1925 & c.1954. Two Dunhills. A "Sports" on the left and a "Baby Sylph" on the right. The Sports is a gold plated over brass model with engine turning. It is an "A" size, also known as a medium size Dunhill, and it has the earlier straight snuffer arm. The Baby Sylph is also gold plate over brass and is less than an inch tall. It has a curved snuffer arm and a double wheel. Value: (L-R) $400-700, $500-1,000.

DUNHILL, c.1925. A Unique model in "B" size with a straight arm snuffer and a single wheel. Ostrich leather on silver plated brass. Value: $60-120.

DUNHILL, c.1926. The lighter on the left is a silver plated "Sports" model with a windshield and the one on the right is a Sterling silver "Unique B" with a nice engine turned design. Value: (L-R) $200-250, $300-350.

DUNHILL, c.1926. A pair of Sterling silver straight arm, single wheel, watch lighters. The one on the left is a "B" size model and the one on the right is an "A" size model. The front opens to gain access to the watch winder. Value: $1,500-2,000.

DUNHILL, c.1929. An English made Dueling Pistol lighter made of brass and a lead alloy. The barrel pulls out to refill. Value: $125-225.

DUNHILL, c.1930. A pair of "Unique Bijou" lighters. The right one is a "Long Bijou" and is slightly longer than the left one. Both are silver plated. Value: $175-225.

DUNHILL, c.1930. A Unique "C" lighter, the largest and hardest to find of the Unique models, in silver plated metal. 2" wide. Value: $500-600.

DUNHILL, c.1934 & 1954. Two Dunhill ruler lighters. The left one is a silver plated over brass "Unique" which measures 1.25" wide. The right one is also silver plated but in a "Sylph" model that is 0.5" wide. Value: (L-R) $300-400, $100-200.

DUNHILL, c.1935. A "Touch-tip" style lighter of gold plating and black lacquer. The rod was depressed in order to position the plunger correctly. One would push the plunger down with the rod to get a light. Then the plunger would be returned to its slot, pressing it down to make it ready for the next use. Value: $1,000-1,200.

DUNHILL, c.1935. A Dunhill-Cartier licensed Japanese "Namiki" "Tallboy" lighter. 3" tall. Value: $1,000-1,400.

DUNHILL, c.1936. Two "Handy" models. On the left is a black enamel over silver plate with Namiki Japanese lacquering. On the right is a Sterling silver model. Value: (L-R) $500-900, $300-500.

DUNHILL, c.1940. The Dunhill "Giant" table lighter. A table version of their popular pocket model. 4" tall. Value: $175-275.

DUNHILL, c.1941. A Japanese decorated Namiki "Squareboy" lighter. The body is Sterling silver and both sides are shown. The maki-e lacquer work is highly sought by collectors. Value: $1,200-1,500.

DUNHILL, c.1942. A Unique "Standard" table lighter made of silver plated brass. Note the internal spring on top to give tension to the snuffer arm. This model was begun during the early 1940s and was referred to as the "Wartime Model Unique." English made, 4" tall. Value: $125-225.

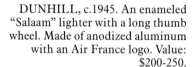

DUNHILL, c.1943. Two Dunhill "Service" lighters. One with an enamel finish and the other in Sterling silver. Value: (L-R) $15, $50.

DUNHILL, c.1945. An enameled "Salaam" lighter with a long thumb wheel. Made of anodized aluminum with an Air France logo. Value: $200-250.

DUNHILL, c. 1944. "Silent Flame" lighters. Made in the USA, they used 2 "C" batteries. On the left is the famous burlesque star Sally Rand. In the center is the woman with a ball and on the right is the sailboat. Value: (L) $40-60, (Ctr & R) $95-150.

DUNHILL, c.1945. An unusual Dunhill "Silent Flame" table lighter with an airplane. It used 2 "C" cell batteries to heat a coil which ignited the wick. Value: $100-200.

DUNHILL, c.1953. The Dunhill "Aquarium" table lighter. Hand painted design with silver plate over brass. 5" wide. Value: $500-1,000.

DUNHILL, c.1947. A "Rollboy" lighter in Sterling silver. Value: $400-500.

DUNHILL, c.1946. A rope style lighter in Sterling silver with its original box. One does not usually equate Dunhill with this primitive style lighter. The rope smoldered rather than creating a flame. This protected the soldier from being seen when he used the lighter. Value: $50-100.

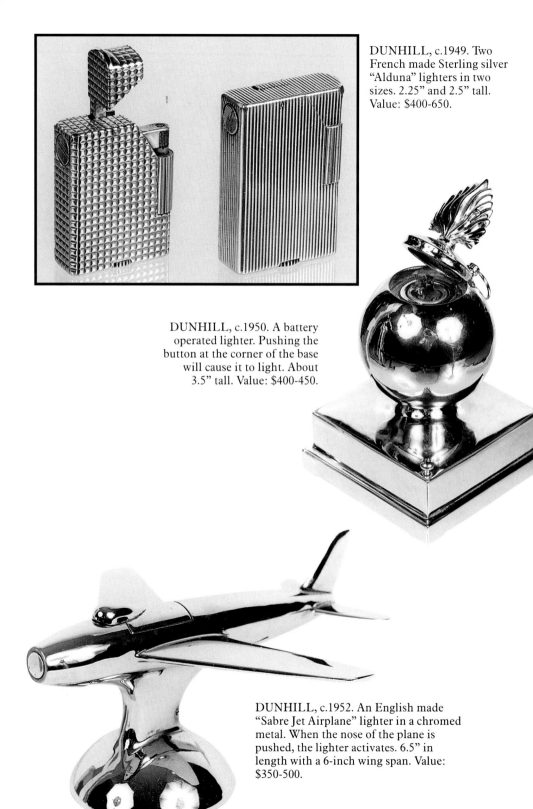

DUNHILL, c.1949. Two French made Sterling silver "Alduna" lighters in two sizes. 2.25" and 2.5" tall. Value: $400-650.

DUNHILL, c.1950. A battery operated lighter. Pushing the button at the corner of the base will cause it to light. About 3.5" tall. Value: $400-450.

DUNHILL, c.1952. An English made "Sabre Jet Airplane" lighter in a chromed metal. When the nose of the plane is pushed, the lighter activates. 6.5" in length with a 6-inch wing span. Value: $350-500.

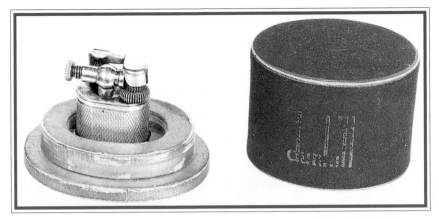

DUNHILL, c.1953. A silver plated, engine turned pattern "Baby Sylph" lighter in its original "top hat" presentation box. This was Dunhill's smallest lighter, standing only 1" tall. Value: $800-1,000 w/box.

DUNHILL, 1960s & 70s. "Rollalite" models. The one on the left is a "Rollagas" and the other three are wick models. Value: $45-85.

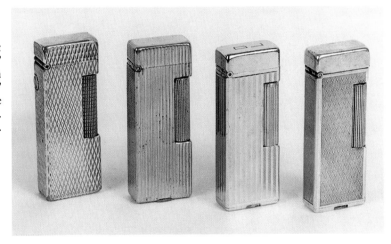

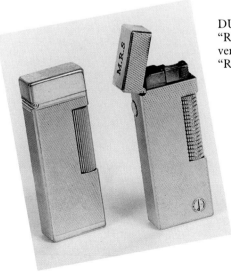

DUNHILL, 1970s. A "Rollagas" model. A gas version of the earlier "Rollalites." Value: $45-85.

DUNHILL, c.1971. A Dunhill "Wheat Sheaf" gas table lighter in gold plated metal. Value: $125-250.

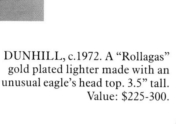

DUNHILL, c.1972. A "Rollagas" gold plated lighter made with an unusual eagle's head top. 3.5" tall. Value: $225-300.

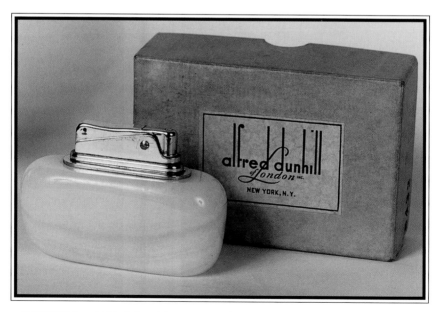

DUNHILL, c.1972. A Dunhill Onyx table butane lighter made in Germany together with its original box. Value: $150-250.

DUPONT, c.1942. An aluminum petrol lighter made in France. It is unusual as far as Duponts go in that it has a small (1/8") thumb wheel on the opposite side. Most Duponts have a longer thumb wheel. Value: $350-475.

ELGIN AMERICAN, c.1952. The lighter has a great cigarette ad for Old Gold. The lighter is valued at about $20 for a plain model but interesting advertising increases the value. Value: $50-60.

ELECTRO-MATCH, c.1965. Two electric lighters made in Hong Kong. It used 3 "AA" batteries and the wick was on the end of the rod. 5" to 6" tall. Value: $35-60.

45

ELGIN-AMERICAN, c.1955. An automatic lighter with a advertisement for RC. Value: $75-100 (w/RCA ad), $20-30 (plain).

ELGIN-OTIS, c.1924. An early American watch lighter from the well-known Elgin Watch Company. Elgin was the watch company and Otis was the lighter company. Watch lighters were made in the 1920s to 1940s. Elgin made a wonderful assortment of Art Deco table lighters as well as the watch lighters. This model has an interesting geared mechanism and is chrome plate over brass. Value: $500-900.

EVANS

Evans or The Evans Case Company, 1922 -1960s, was located in North Attleborough, Massachusetts. They began business by making handbag accessories. About 1928 they started manufacturing cigarette lighters. Their earliest models were the lift arm lighters. Evans continued to make this style lighter until about 1930.

Their first automatic lighter, named according to its purpose, was introduced about 1929. The "Automatic" is usually differentiated by the "shoulder" construction. The shoulder is the top center of the lighter between the push button or lever and the snuffer. Looking from the side, the shoulder of the "Automatic" had an old tombstone shape. It was symmetrical, rounded on top, and then sloped down to another smaller shoulder.

Their next automatic lighter was the "Roller Bearing Action" lighter with the bulk of these being made from about 1932 through 1934. Their shoulders were symmetrical, with a flattened top, slopping down to the lighter body.

Following the Roller Bearing was the "Trig-a-lite." Their symmetrical shoulder had a flattened top and rounded sides that went almost straight down without a slope. They were made from about 1934 to about 1940. There were actually a few Trig-a-lites made with Roller Bearing shoulders in the late 1930s.

The "Spitfire" model (an unofficial name) followed the Trig-a-lite, which was then followed by the "Banner" model. Spitfires were first made about 1940 and are characterized by the non-symmetrical sloping shoulder (what we call the typical Evan's look) with large screws in the side of the shoulder. The "Banner" had the same shape shoulders, but replaced the screws with pins or hid them completely. A taller, slimmer Banner was called the "Supreme." The "Banner" model is the lighter most easily recognized as an Evans.

Evans also made a "Clipper" model which did not have a push button or lever sticking up from the end opposite the snuffer. There were also a few other models and style variations within each model.

Gas models were made toward the end of the company's existence.

EVANS, c.1928. A pair of lift arm Evans lighters. One with elephant skin leather and the other with lizard skin leather. 3" tall.
Value: $60-75.

Opposite page:
Bottom left: ESPRIT, c.1950. A handsome 14kt gold, German made lighter. Esprit lighters are hard to find and one in 14kt gold is very rare. Value: $500-600.

Bottom center: ETERNA, c.1926. A Sterling silver lighter with a Swiss watch. Eterna is still in business making watches today and makes a very high quality product. Value: $900-1400.

Bottom right: ETERNA, c.1935. A Sterling silver lighter with a watch in its side. This was made in Switzerland. 2.5" tall. Value: $1,200-1,500.

EVANS, c.1929. A pair of early lift arm Evans lighters. The tall one is leather covered and the short one is enameled. Currently, in the standard size, enameled models are more valuable. 3" and 5.5" tall. Value: $200-300.

EVANS, c.1930. An oversized silver plated Evans lift arm lighter. Value: $40-75.

EVANS, c.1932. An Evans "Roller Bearing." The Roller Bearing was a beautiful series of cloisonné enameled Art Deco pocket lighters. They are actively sought by collectors. Value: $300-400.

EVANS, c.1932. A handsome Art Deco "Roller Bearing" lighter with two color enamel on a nickel or chrome plated brass. Value: $100-200.

EVANS, c.1937. A beautiful Evans combination compact, "Trig-a-lite" lighter, and cigarette case in an Art Deco enamel finish. Even though the cigarettes were separated from the powder in the compact, they still would taste like powder. These combinations were attractive and available in many patterns and color combinations. They were produced into the 1940s. Value: $150-250.

EVANS, c.1933. A cigarette case with a built-in "Roller Bearing" lighter. Chrome plated with a geometric design in black and white enamel. Value: $200-250.

EVANS, c.1938. A trio of "Trig-A-Lite" table lighters. About 2.5" to 4" tall. Value: $100-150 each.

EVANS, c.1939. An Evans ball table lighter. This model has a "Trig-a-lite" mechanism and is 3" in diameter. Value: $75-125.

EVANS, c.1945. A small sized American Sterling silver "Petite" lighter. 2" tall. Value: $150-200.

EVANS, c.1948. A pair of Evans lighters made for a woman's purse in two sizes: a "Petite" and a "Banner." Needlepoint covered on the left and mother-of-pearl covered on the right. 1.75" and 2.5" tall. Value: $25-35.

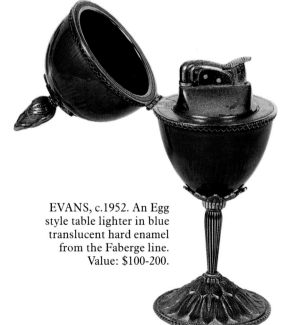

EVANS, c.1951. An antiqued copper table lighter with a rampant lion design. Value: $25-45.

EVANS, c.1952. An Egg style table lighter in blue translucent hard enamel from the Faberge line. Value: $100-200.

EVANS, c.1952. Two Evans table lighters in the shape of a Genie Lamp. Value: $20-40.

EVANS, c.1952. A small Evans table lighter in the shape of a flying saucer. It is made of a nickel plated brass. Value: $20-40.

EVANS, c.1952. A Wedgwood table lighter. Value: $30-50.

EVANS, c.1952. A table lighter with a transfer design on white porcelain. Value: $20-40.

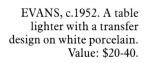

EVANS, c.1954. Valerie is holding a "Sophistacase" lady's purse that contains everything that a lady might need. In addition to a cigarette lighter, there are two lipsticks, a compact, a change purse, two mirrors, a comb, and an extra compartment to carry whatever the Sophistacase forgot to include. Made in the U.S. 5.75" x 3.5". Value: $150-200.

EVANS, c.1954. Two Evans table lighters in the shape of a flying saucer. Value: $20-40.

EVANS, c.1954. The beauty of Evans "Banner" style lighters is that they usually have a distinctive Evans' look. This is no exception; but it is better looking than most. It is Sterling silver and a one piece design (lighter is not removable) with the flint screw and filler screw on the bottom. Value: $50-90.

EVANS, c.1955. "Clearfloat" lighters made by the Evans Case Co. in Massachusetts. 4" and 7" tall. Value: $25-65.

EVEREST, c.1933. A Sterling silver lighter and a 14kt gold model both with engine turned designs. The Everest was made in England. Value: (L-R) $200-250, $400-500.

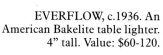

EVERFLOW, c.1936. An American Bakelite table lighter. 4" tall. Value: $60-120.

EWEOL, c.1915. A German pocket lighter with the barest of parts. It has a flint wheel and a small fluid container into which the wick goes. Its mechanism is unusual since it spins to create the spark. The knurled part of the rod is spun to turn the flint wheel. Value: $175-250.

FEUDOR, c.1943. A model "100" French lift arm lighter. Chrome plated brass with a nice Art Deco engine turned design. Value: $60-90.

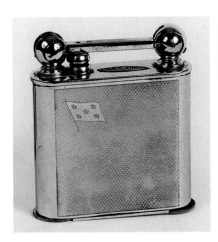

FLAMIDOR, c.1936. This French chrome plated table lighter is operated by squeezing the ball on the right side. This releases the arm and produces the flame. 4" tall. Value: $125-225.

FLAMIDOR, c.1936. A French made automatic lighter in Sterling silver. Value: $200-250.

FLAMIDOR, c.1939. A French made lighter of celluloid covered aluminum. The advertisement is for LeClanche Batteries. LeClanche is one of the oldest battery companies. Notice the vertical flint wheel often seen on French made lighters of this time. Value: $40-80.

FUMALUX, c.1960. A German made, chrome electric lighter with a built-in flashlight. When the slide is pulled back, the top opens and a hot wire lights the wick. The button works the flashlight. It uses a small, difficult to find battery. 2.25" wide. Value: $25-35.

GALTON, c.1965. This Metuchen, New Jersey, made electric lighter plugs into the wall for recharging. 3" tall. Value: $25-45.

GEM, c.1933. A great looking celluloid covered lighter with a vertically mounted flint wheel. Value: $75-125.

GOLDEN WHEEL, c.1924. Man's lift arm pocket lighter. This is good quality lighter. Golden Wheel was American made from the 1920s to about 1940. Golden Wheel made a very broad range of lighters—from the cheap trinket to high quality lighters. This is an unusual 8-sided model. Value: $40-80.

GOLDEN WHEEL, c.1937. A seldom seen "Golden Wheel" model in brushed Sterling silver. Value: $225-275.

GO-LIGHT, c.1937. An unusual design silver plated, English made lighter. Value: $200-250.

HAHWAY, c.1914. A silver plated lighter made in Germany. When the button is pushed, the top opens and the lighter lights. 3" tall. Value: $40-50.

HAHWAY, c.1916. A superb Hahway lighter made in Bavaria. The image of the 3 people in the old car is hand engraved. Button on the right side is pushed and the lighter opens lit. The filler screw has a ring attached so that the lighter could be worn on a chain. A lighter with such a good early engraving will also be sought by car collectors who may pay more than a lighter collector. Value: $250-350.

HAHWAY, c.1925. This most unusual Sterling silver lighter had space inside for a photograph. 2.75" tall. Value: $550-750.

HAMILTON, c.1942. An airplane lighter made in the United States. Turn the propeller and the cockpit opens with a flame. It is unusual to find in white; it is more commonly found in chrome. 4" tall. Value: $100-145.

HAMILTON, c.1948. While not an unusual lighter, this baked blue enamel finish is unusual to find. The lighter lights when the propeller is turned. Value: $100-125.

HARVEY AVEDON, c.1952. A modern design lighter in 14kt gold. Value: $400-450.

H.L. LTD, c.1925. An English made lighter with an enamel on hallmarked Sterling silver. Perhaps a prized pilot's lighter with his flight wings insignia. 2.5" tall. Value: $350-450.

HOLD HEET, c.1936. An unusual table lighter that looks similar to an old fashioned candlestick telephone. This model is called the Electric Match Lighter. It plugs into a wall outlet, and, when the red button is pushed, the coil heats up. 7" tall. Value: $80-120.

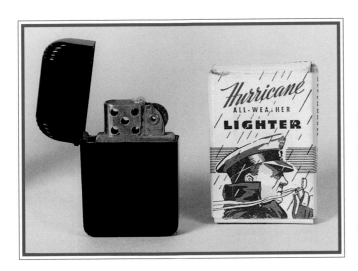

HURRICANE, c.1939. An interesting inexpensive Bakelite lighter with its original box. Made in Bradford, Pennsylvania, by Rathburn and patented in 1931, just before Zippo, which was located in the same town. 2.5" tall. Value: $40-75 (w/ box).

IMCO, c.1928. An unusual looking IMCO lighter in chrome over brass and with a windguard. IMCO lighters were made or imported in the 1960s by The IMCO Manufacturing Corp., 541 Avenue of the Americas, New York City. In the 1960s, they made a series of narrow upright pocket lighter models called the "Junior," "Regular," "Super," and "Streamline" as well as a gun shaped lighter called the "Gunlite." The "Gunlite" was a "Super" lighter turned on its side with a gun grip and trigger. It is believed that the 1960s lighters were all made in Austria for IMCO. 2.5" tall. Value: $125-175.

IMPACT, c.1971. A gold plated Zippo style lighter with an AFL-CIO medallion. This was a souvenir of the 1971 conference. Value: $15-25.

ITHACA, c.1918. A nice combination lighter/mechanical pencil in the shape of a champagne bottle. It was called a waiter's pencil since it could light your cigarette as well as write your order. Value: $40-75.

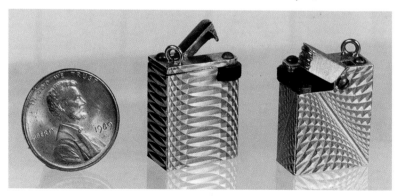

Jewelry, c.1950. Two 9kt gold lighter charms that might hang from a charm bracelet. The penny is shown to compare size.

Jewelry, c.1950. One 18kt gold lighter and two gold filled lighter charms for a charm bracelet. The 18kt gold one on the left has a ruby heart where the wick would be. The penny is shown to compare size.

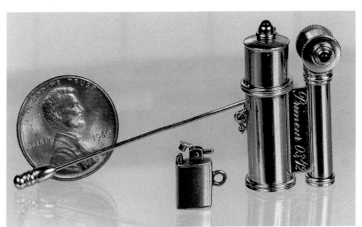

Jewelry, c.1950. The tiny lighter on the left is a 14kt gold lighter charm for a charm bracelet. The piece on the right is an 18kt gold stickpin with small rubies in the top. It is a working miniature lighter of which only 12 were made. The penny is shown to compare size.

Jewelry, c.1950. Two Dunhill lift arm lighter charms, one 9kt gold and one Sterling silver, for a charm bracelet. The penny is shown to compare size.

Jewelry, c.1950. Two tiny working striker lighter charms, one is silver and enamel and the other is silver, that might hang from a charm bracelet. The penny is shown to compare size.

Jewelry, c.1950. A group of lighter charms that might hang from a charm bracelet. With the exception of the leather covered one, they open and reveal a tiny pipe or cigarette and ashtray. The penny is shown to compare size.

Jewelry, c.1950. A pair of Sterling silver cufflinks in the shape of lighters. The penny is shown to compare size.

Jewelry, c.1950. Two pair of earrings in the shape of lighters. One is gold plated with green lacquer and the other resembles a pair of Sterling silver Zippo lighters The penny is shown to compare size.

Jewelry, c.1950. A group of four charms in the shape of lighters. The penny is shown to compare size.

Jewelry, c.1962. Three lighter charms for a charm bracelet. The lighter to far right is 9kt gold and enamel. The penny is shown to compare size.

JOHNNY D.L., c.1933. A Japanese lighter with an Egyptian design on its side. It has an unusual flint adjustment wheel on top. Value: $150-200.

KABLO, c.1940. A smaller pocket lighter made in Czechoslovakia. It has a Sterling silver overlay. Value: $60-100.

K50, c.1940. This German made lighter has a safety feature. You must press both sides to make it light. The Berkel name is an advertisement. Value: $150-200.

KASCHIE, c.1935. A Sterling silver Kaschie side push lighter. 2" tall. Value: $275-375.

KASCHIE, c.1933. A great German lighter with a car's radiator shape. When the ball switch on the right is pushed down, the top opens and the lighter lights. Silver plate with machine engraving. Value: $200-250.

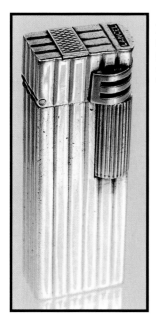

LANCEL, c.1940. A silver plated lighter with an interesting rounded windguard design. Value: $200-250.

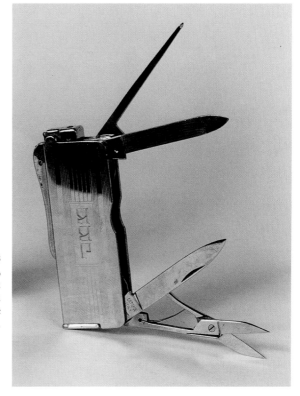

LATIMA, c.1954. A great Swiss Army style lighter and knife. Blades, scissors, punch, and a lighter in chrome metal. Lighter was made in Austria with the blades being made in Italy. Value: $75-125.

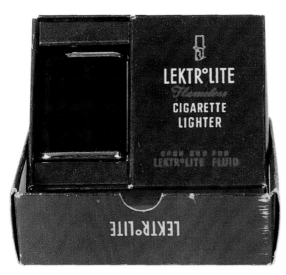

LEKTROLITE, c.1935. A Bakelite lighter that used chemicals to create the flame rather than a flint and wheel. If all worked right, the lighter would light when the combustion area was exposed to the air. Value: $40-80.

LEKTROLITE, c.1935. The Lektrolite chemical lighter used a special fluid which was supposed to light upon exposure to air. The body of the lighter is a Bakelite plastic. 1.5" tall. Value: $75-100 (w/box).

LE MONDIAL, c.1925. A Swiss made lift arm lighter with an unusual horizontal flint wheel where the flint is under the wheel. 2.75" tall. Value: $200-250.

LITTLE GEM, c.1888. The Little Gem is an early fulminate of mercury (a chemical combination) cap lighter. When a lever on the side was pushed down, the wheel spun and a pin struck the cap causing the spark to light the wick. Value: $250-350.

LUX, c.1933. A "Trik" model lighter made in Germany. Chrome plate with black enamel. Value: $100-150.

MAGICIENNE, c.1900. A wonderful match dispenser lighter. When the rod was pushed in, the match would be pushed out and lit as a result of scraping against a sharp tip. Value: $200-300.

MAGIC POCKET LAMP, c.1889. A hard-to-find early pocket lighter called Koopman's Magic Pocket Lamp. It used the fulminate of mercury caps that were first used during the American Civil War. Pushing a button on the side would cause a wheel to turn, moving the cap into place to be struck by a metal pin and creating a spark to ignite the wick. Value: $125-200.

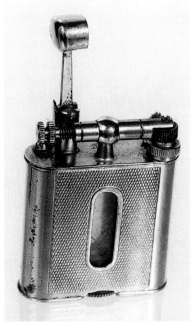

MANO, c.1935. A European lift arm lighter which may have been the first "view" lighter made. Silver plate with an engine turned finish. Value: $150-200.

MARATHON, c.1925. An American made—located in North Attleborough, Mass.—lighter with a great hump shaped windguard. Marathon lighters (1915 to 1940s) are highly sought after being of very high quality. The earliest ones (pre-1925) are highly prized, as are the cigarette case/ lighter combinations. 2.75" tall. Value: $175-225.

71

MARATHON, c.1935. An Art Deco lift arm lighter with two color enamel on nickel. 2.5" tall. Value: $175-250.

Center: MASTER-LITE, c.1917. An old store display of pocket lighters with a great advertising cover. "No Wind Can Blow It Out" was the selling point. Value: $300-400 (full box).

Bottom & opposite page, top: MB, c.1917. The Manning-Bowman & Co. Tobacco-Lighter is an electric cigarette lighter that was made in Meriden, Connecticut. It was patented in 1911. Shown with its box. Value: $100-150.

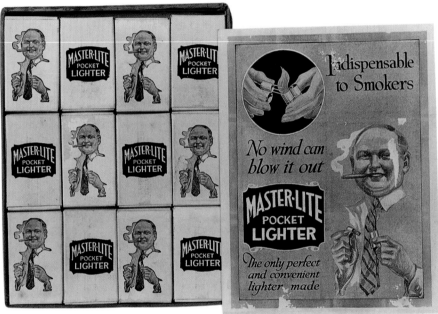

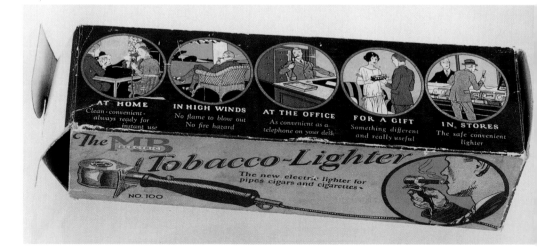

MCMURDO, c.1936. A great looking Art Deco table lighter with an unusual thumb roller positioned on the top. The roller is connected to the snuff arm and lifts it. 7" tall. Value: $125-225.

MCMURDO, c.1938. Art Deco style lighter in chrome. Made in England. Has an unusual side-mounted thumb roller. Value: $50-100.

MEB, c.1930. The Meb Austrian lighter is contained in two Art Deco metal animals. Value: $100-125 each.

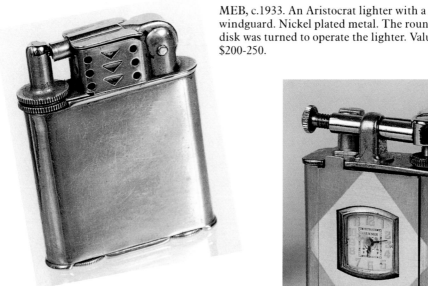

MEB, c.1933. An Aristocrat lighter with a windguard. Nickel plated metal. The round disk was turned to operate the lighter. Value: $200-250.

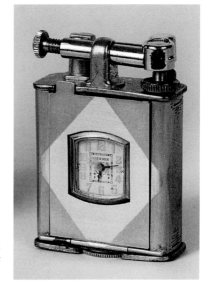

MONROE, c.1922. A watch lighter made of chrome and zinc alloy. Value: $90-175.

MONROE, c.1923. A U.S. made
watch chrome plated lighter
with a diamond shaped watch.
Value: $100-175.

MOUCHON, c.1937. A French made
enameled chrome plated lighter with an Art
Deco design. When the sides were pushed
in, the top would open and the lighter would
light. Value: $250-300.

MUGETTE, c.1935. A small
Bakelite lighter made to look like
a miniature camera. Made in
Germany. 2.5" tall. Value: $75-100.

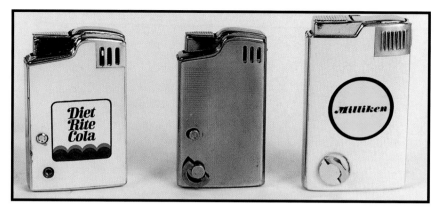

Musical, 1950s. Three musical Japanese made lighters, two with advertising. There was a small winding screw at the bottom front that wound the music box mechanism. The music would start when the lighter was lit. One tune was "Smoke Gets In Your Eyes." Value: $50-125.

MYCRAFT, c.1964. A wind up musical pocket lighter with a poodle design. The opposite side has the winding key. Japanese made. The music would start every time you lit the lighter. Value: $50-75.

MYFLAM, c.1955. A German made semi-automatic table lighter. It has a silver sleeve. Very often, these German pieces have a beer fest or tavern scene on them. 4" tall. Value: $40-60.

NASCO, c.1925. An engine turned lift arm lighter with the image of a soccer player on the side. 2.5" tall. Value: $200-250.

NEGBAUR, c.1942. The "Mystic Torch" made by Negbaur in New York. A Bakelite plastic electric lighter with a battery inside. The knob had a wick at the opposite end. 4" tall. Value: $60-85.

NEGBAUR, c.1948. An American made golf bag shaped lighter. Made of a pot metal. To light it, you would push the head of the golf club on the right. 5" tall. Value: $50-75.

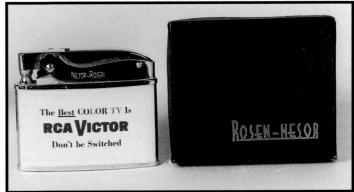

NESOR-ROSEN, c.1968. The box says Rosen-Nesor and the lighter says Nesor-Rosen. Whatever you wish to call it, it is a neat advertising piece for the RCA Color Television. Value: $35-70.

NETOP, 1920s. The Netop had an unusual and compact flint wheel, wick, and snuffer. When the little ball was pulled back, it would uncap the snuffer, then spark and light. The flint wheel is vertically mounted. Value: $50-90.

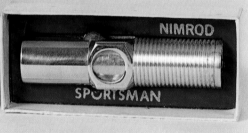

NIMROD, c.1955. The Nimrod Sportsman pipe lighter in aluminum metal with original packaging. Value: $25-45 (w/ box).

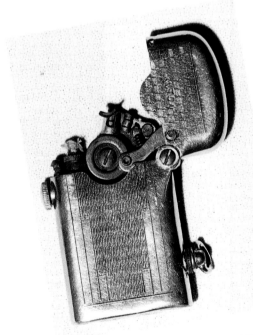

NUTON, c.1918. An early semi-automatic pocket lighter that resembles a Thorens, but is much more complex. Value: $300-400.

Occupied Japan, c.1945. A cowboy lighter in chrome plated metal. When you pulled back his head, the lighter was exposed. 3" tall. Value: $40-60.

The Japanese lighter industry grew dramatically in the 1950s and 1960s. Several American companies took advantage of the cheap labor in Japan and set up cigarette lighter factories. Japanese lighters made between 1945 and 1952 were stamped "Made in Occupied Japan." After the occupation, Japanese lighter manufacturers began producing thousands of models of lighters. By the end of the 1960s, the quality was among the best that could be found worldwide. Japan led the world in lighter innovation in the 1970s.

Occupied Japan, c.1945. A Buddha lighter. A fairly common lighter with a removable insert. Value: $20-30.

Occupied Japan, c.1946. The Leader lighter looked like a radio. It was a combination lighter and cigarette dispenser. The white knob operated the lighter and the black knob dispensed a cigarette. Top is removed to load cigarettes and they were dispensed from the left side. Value: $200-300.

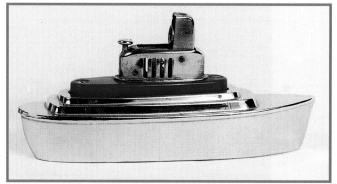

Occupied Japan, c.1948. A table lighter in the shape of a boat. The boat is chrome plated brass with a red Bakelite accent. 5" long. Value: $75-125.

Occupied Japan, c.1948. A lighter in the shape of a camera, with a working compass on its face. The lighter also has a safety switch to prevent accidental lighting. 3.5" tall. Value: $45-70.

Occupied Japan, c.1948. A pair of lighters in the shape of a camera. The lighter on the right has a movable zoom lens. 3.5" tall. Value: (L-R) $45-70, $100-150.

Occupied Japan, c.1949. A pair of Japanese made golf ball shaped lighters in chrome metal. The one on the left has a built-in windscreen. About 2.5" tall. Value: $75-100.

Occupied Japan, c.1949. A tiny lighter only 1 inch tall in the shape of a miniature camera. A penny is shown for size comparison. Made in Occupied Japan. Value: $200-300.

Occupied Japan, c.1950. White metal cowboy boot lighters. 4" tall. Value: $20-45.

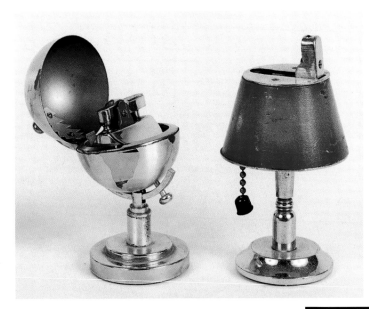

Occupied Japan, c.1952. Two Japanese lighters. The one on the right is in the shape of a globe (a matching cigarette dispenser was also available) and the one on the right, marked "Occupied Japan," is shaped like a lamp. 5" tall. Value: (L-R) $20-40, $40-70.

ORLIK, c.1922. A nickel plated brass lighter with an ostrich leather covering. This was a well made early windproof lighter. Orlik, founded in 1899, began as a pipe maker. They moved on to making lighters about 1916, some of which were made in the U.S. and others in the U.K. Their lighters seem to disappear in the 1940s. Value: $75-110.

ORLIK, c.1925. An English "Matchless" model lighter with a wonderful foot shaped snuffer cap. 2.5" tall. Value: $100-150.

ORLIK, c.1928. An Orlik standard sized lighter in Sterling silver. It was made in England. 2.75" tall. Value: $350-450.

ORLIK, c.1926. An English lighter with an unusually positioned flint wheel in front of the wick. Leather covered and nickel plated metal. Value: $200-250.

PARK USA, c.1944. Zippo look-a-likes with a crinkle paint finish. Value: $25-35.

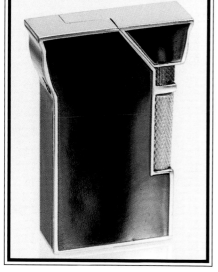

PAM, c.1940. A French made gold plate and enameled lighter with an unusual top end. It flares out rather than having straight sides. Value: $200-250.

83

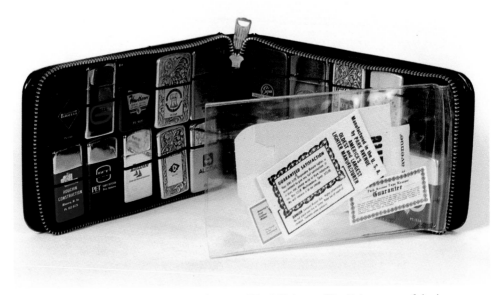

PARK, c.1954. A full salesman's sample case of Park lighters. The lighters are of the inexpensive advertising type. The beauty of this item is that it shows an assortment of styles and decoration. Value: $250-350.

PARK, c.1964. A Zippo style pocket lighter with a Ready Kilowatt advertising image on the side. Value: $40-60.

PARK, c.1964. A Zippo-style lighter that was made in the USA. This is a particularly wonderful example with an ad for the Park lighter on the side of the case. Value: $100-125.

PARKER, c.1935. Two Sterling silver Parker "Beacon" lift arm lighters. The one on the left has a full body length wheel to strike the spark. 2.5" and 2.75" tall. Value: $200-250 ea.

PARKER, c.1935. An English made "Roller Beacon" table lighter. A finely made lift arm in a silver plated brass with engine turning. The little arm on top of the snuffer arm was a nice touch that would prevent your fingers from picking up any soot left on the snuffer. Value: $150-250.

PARROT, c. 1965. The flashlight with a cigarette lighter. A red switch on the side uncovers and turns on a small hot coil just below the lens. Made in Hong Kong. 7" tall. Value: $20-$30.

PENGUIN, c.1952. A souvenir of Illinois—the Land of Lincoln. Typical of the Japanese souvenir lighters of this time. Value: $20-30.

PHINNEY WALKER, c.1928. A table clock lighter with an automatic action. Push the button and it opens lit. 4" tall. Value: $100-150.

PHINNEY WALKER, c.1946. This brass table clock has a built-in Evans lighter. 4" tall. Value: $65-150.

PIP-CIG, c.1936. A nice Art Deco silver plated lighter with a windguard. It is decorated with an engine turned design with engraving. Value: $100-150.

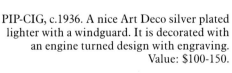

PLAZA, 1940s. An unusual compact shaped lighter. It looks like a lady's compact, but when opened, it lights. Probably not what you would want to give to an inebriated lady. Value: $50-125.

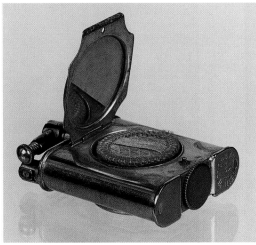

POLLACK, c.1928. A lift arm Art Deco lighter. This model has two mirrored compacts, one on each side. One holds powder and the other rouge. This was made in the U.S. 2.5" tall. Value: $300-400.

POPEYE, c.1984. A Japanese figural lighter of Popeye. Turning his arm shoots a gas flame out from his pipe. 3.5" tall. Value: $35-60.

POPPEL, c.1965. An early gas Bakelite lighter made in the Netherlands. 3" tall. Value: $60-90 (w/box).

PREMIER, c.1925. An English silver plated automatic lighter. 2.5" tall. Value: $175-250.

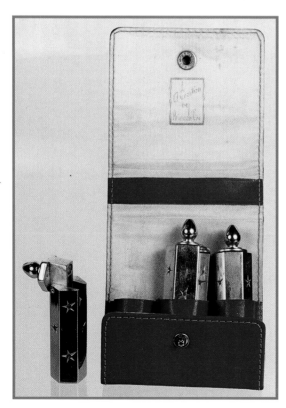

PRESEN CO., c.1935. A lady's three piece set of lipstick, perfume, and lighter all in a leather case. 3" tall. Value: $100-150.

PRESS-A-LITE, c.1931. A
Touch-tip style lighter of green
plastic and chrome. About 4"
tall. Value: $150-200.

QUERCIA
(FLAMINAIRE), c.1948.
A Sterling Silver French
made Quercia
Flaminaire lighter with
its original box.
Flaminaire was a
French firm that
made the first gas
lighter. Manufactur-
ing rights were
owned by the
Quercia family who
owned the
Flamidor company
that had been making
lighters just after the turn of the
century. Marcel Quercia improved a model invented
by Henri Pingeot in 1936. The first commercial gas table lighter,
the Gentry, was introduced in June, 1947. It was a very expensive lighter when
first introduced. In 1948, they brought out the Crillon—named after the hotel where it was
introduced—which was the first pocket model. The company did well and the lighter was
well received. The lighter used a unique gas cartridge that only it was able to produce. This
kept the price high. The first automatic gas lighter was the Galet that came out in 1959. Its
gas tank was replaceable. Value: $100-150 (silver), $30-45 (plated), $60-90 (enameled).

QUERCIA (FLAMINAIRE), c.1950. The Flaminaire was made by Quercia in France. The American rights to distribute the lighter were purchased by the Parker Pen Company. This brass counter top store display is a great looking piece. Value: $200-250.

QUERCIA (FLAMINAIRE), c.1950. French made butane table lighter. This is one of the first butane pocket lighters that used a disposable tank. The entire tank was replaced when empty. Parker Pen Company of Janesville, Wisconsin, believed that cigarette lighters were a good companion product for their fountain pen business. They obtained the rights to sell the lighter in the United States. Sales were poor as the gas cartridges were not refillable and were expensive compared to non-gas models. They quickly closed out that portion of their business. Value: $30-45.

R & G, c.1932. A two piece lighter and cigarette case set, silver plated metal in its original case. The lighter is unusual in that it has a recessed area for the wick and also a hinged lid that opens toward the back. R & G made a lot of women's accessories like Evans. Value: $200-300.

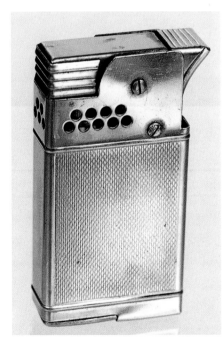

RAPID, c.1935. An Austrian made lighter. Chrome plate with an engine turned finish. Value: $100-150.

RAZZIA, c.1946. A nicely made black Bakelite gun shaped lighter that also stores cigarettes in the grip. Squeezing the trigger once opens the compartment; the second squeeze lights the lighter. Value: $50-100.

R.B. CO., c.1952. The R. Blackington vermeil lighter was made in America. Vermeil is gold plated Sterling silver. 2" tall. Value: $200-300.

REVOLT, c.1922. An Austrian made lighter with an engine turned pattern with hand engraved embellishment. It is very nice due to the area on the front made to hold a photograph. Value: $150-200.

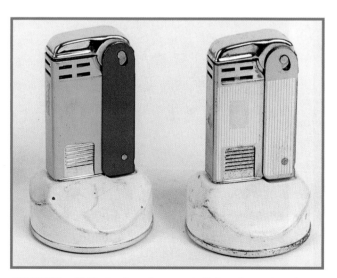

REGENS, c.1946. An American made lighter in a painted enamel over brass. While these look like table lighters, the brass base is the original store display base. Value: $50-75.

RITEPOINT, c.1954. A nice mint in the box model with a Time-Life magazine advertising insert. Both sides are shown. Rite-Point was also a maker of mechanical pencils and pens. Value: $50-80.

RITEPOINT, c.1954. Two sizes of Ritepoint lighters. Value: $25-40.

RITEPOINT, c.1954. This is a nice mint in the box model with a Chesterfield cigarettes ad insert. Value: $75-125.

RITEPOINT, c.1958. A table lighter with visible fuel tank containing an advertisement. Rite-Point was a precursor to Scripto. 3.5" tall. Value: $40-60.

ROLLS ENFIELD, c.1925. An English silver plated kick start (like the Colibri Original) automatic lighter. 2.5" tall. Value: $100-200.

RONSON

Ronson was started before the turn of the century by Louis V. Aronson (1870-1940) as the Art Metal Works of Newark, New Jersey. In the 1920s, they used the name Ronson. It was changed to Ronson Art Metal Works, Inc. in 1945, and later became the Ronson Corporation in 1954. Their first pocket lighter in 1913 was called the "Wonderliter." It was a wand or striker type lighter. (Because these wands may have been lost and replaced over time, collectors need to know what these should look like. They should fit snugly in their hole.) Ronson's first striker pencil lighter appeared in 1919. Their first automatic cigar lighter (patented in 1918, but introduced in 1926-1927) was called the "Banjo:" 'automatic' meaning that one push would expose the wick, turn the striking wheel, and light the lighter. After the "Banjo" came the "Standard" (1928) and then the "Princess" (1929), which was smaller and made for about 30 years. The "Standard" and other early lighters were marked "Ronson De-light." These used a screw that passed through the fulcrum from one side and screwed into the other side of the lighter mechanism. Later they used two screws, one entering from each side of the lighter to hold the mechanism. Introduced in 1947, the "Adonis" model, designed by Frederick Kaupmann, was made for about 20 years. The first butane models appeared in the early 1950s.

RONSON, c.1927. The Banjo lighter with box and instructions. The Banjo was the first automatic lighter and was patented in 1918, but not produced until 1927. 4" tall. Value: $500-900.

RONSON, c.1927. Two "Tabourettes" model lighters. The left one has a standard fitment and the one on the right has a De-light fitment. Chrome and silver plate. 4" tall. Value: $100-200.

RONSON, c.1928. A De-light lighter in the "Standard" size, but in Sterling silver with a nice engine turned design. Value: $275-350.

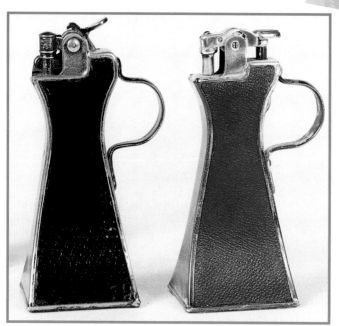

RONSON, c.1928. Two table lighters. A "Tablelighter" on the left with a Banjo mechanism and the one on the right has a De-light mechanism. Nickel plate and leather. 4.625" tall, 2.5" wide. Value: $175-275.

RONSON, c.1928. Two piece De-light Jr. set. Black enamel with marcasite highlights. 2.5" tall. Value: $600-800.

RONSON, c.1928. An unusual, early nickel "Frat" De-light lighter with two different colored leathers. 2.5" tall. Value: $100-150.

RONSON, c.1929. Ronson "Princess Windbreak" lighters with windguards. Chrome plated brass. 2" tall. Value: $100-200.

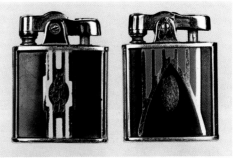

RONSON, c.1929. "Princess" lighters. Two tone lacquered chrome over brass. This was the longest produced Ronson model, almost 30 years. 2" tall. Value: $35-65.

RONSON, c.1929. A group of great Art Deco "Princess" De-light lighters. Chrome and enamel. These were made well into the 1930s. 2" tall. Value: $100-200.

RONSON, c.1929. An unusual lighter called the "Bridge Lighter." Chrome and leather. 3" tall. Value: $150-250.

RONSON, c.1929. A "Superba" table lighter. An Art Deco lighter with a great design. The top fitment is the same as that of the Ronson "Standard." Chrome plate. 5" tall. Value: $500-700.

RONSON, c.1930. A "New Yorker Home Lighter and Ashtray," first introduced in 1930. Gold plate and porcelain. Available in this yellow cream colored onyx or in a pink cream color. 4.25" in diameter. Value: $300-450.

RONSON, c.1930. A "Ballerina" table lighter with ashtray. Chrome and enamel with a New Yorker fitment. It originally had a glass ashtray. 7" tall. Value: $800-1,200.

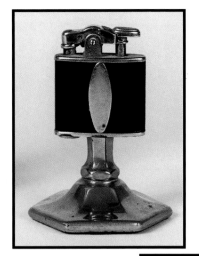

RONSON, c.1930. A painted "Bogey" De-light golf ball lighter. 2.5" tall. Value: $200-300.

RONSON, c.1930. A nickel plated De-light "Standard Tablelighter." A very rare model. 5" tall. Value: $500-600.

RONSON, c.1931. Two "Jumbo Junior" model lighters. Chrome finish. 1.75" tall. Value: $100-200.

RONSON, c.1931. A "Lite-A-Lamp" lighter. The ring is the filler screw. Chrome and enamel. 3.5" tall. Value: $600-800.

RONSON, c.1932. A nice Ronson "Standard" De-light lighter with a motor car on the side. 2.5" tall. Value: $85-145.

RONSON, c.1931. A "Baronet" model lighter with a New Yorker fitment. Chrome and painted white metal. 3" tall. Value: $400-600.

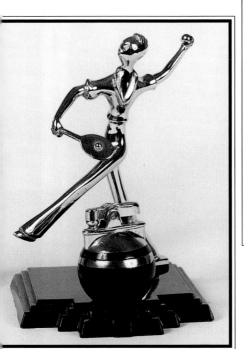

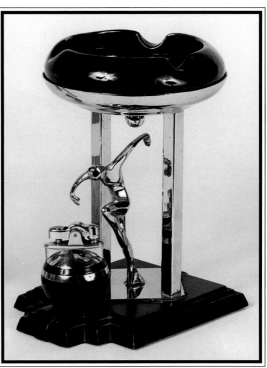

RONSON, c.1932. A "Rondelight Dancer With Ashtray." Chrome and enamel. Used a "Baby Rondelight Ball" lighter. 6" tall. Value: $1,500-2,000.

RONSON, c.1932. A Tennis Player with a "Rondelight" ball lighter. Chrome with a gunmetal base. About 5.5" tall. Value: $1,200-1,750.

RONSON, c.1934. Watch lighters. Gold and silver plated metal with enamel highlights. 3.5" tall. Value: (L-R) $500-700, $400-600.

RONSON, c.1934. De-light lighter. Chrome with silver and black enamel. 2" tall. Value: $350-550.

RONSON, c.1934. De-light lighters. Nickel plate and leather. 2.5" tall. Value: $55-80.

RONSON, c.1934. The "Ace" lighter (similar to a "Rondette Junior" only larger). Chrome with brown enamel. 2.5" tall. Value: $60-90.

RONSON, c.1934. "Banker" lighter. Gold plated. 3" tall. Value: $35-60.

RONSON, c.1934. "Banker" lighter. Enameled scene with a Sterling silver jacket. 3" tall. Value: $200-300.

RONSON, c.1934.
A chrome "Banker"
lighter. 2.125" tall.
Value: $50-75.

RONSON, c.1934. A
"Duchess" table lighter.
Dureum plating on an engine
turned body with a swirl
decorated top and bottom.
3.5" tall. Value: $150-250.

RONSON, c.1934.
"Duplex" lighter.
Chrome with leather.
This is an unusual
model in which the
bottom pulls out for
refueling. These
models are always
found having two
colors, with the top
and bottom the same
and the center band a
different color. 3"
tall. Value: $150-225.

RONSON, c.1934. "Gem" lighter. 3"
tall. Chrome plated brass with enamel.
Value: $35-50.

RONSON, c.1934.
"Fine Line" lighter.
2" tall. The unusual
feature of this
lighter is that the
front and back
panels extend to a
small flat side. It is
more common to
find those sides
rounded. Value:
$100-200.

RONSON, c.1934. "Gem"
lighters. Dureum and black
and rhinestones on chrome.
3" tall. Value: (L-R) $50-90,
$40-60.

RONSON, c.1934. "Gem" lighters. Enamel on the left and shagreen (sharkskin) on the right. 3" tall. Value: $25-40.

RONSON, c.1934. "Junior Sports" lighter made in England. 9kt gold. 3" tall. Value: $650-900.

RONSON, c.1934. "Junior Sports" lighters. Two tone lacquered chrome on the left and gold plate on the right. 3" tall. Value: $75-110.

RONSON, c.1929. Delight lighter. Chrome plate. 3" tall. Value: $75-110.

RONSON, c.1934. "Majorette" lighter. The "Majorette" is similar to the "Regal" only it is a bit larger. Silver plated. 3.5" tall. Value: $400-550.

RONSON, c.1934. "Princess" lighters. The left is silver plated and the right is Sterling silver. 3" tall. Value: (L-R) $40-60, $140-180.

RONSON, c.1934. "Pet" lighters. Chrome with two tone enamel. The "Pet" model is a very Art Deco looking lighter. 3" tall. Value: $100-200.

RONSON, c.1934. Two "Princess" lighters. Gold plate and Chrome. 2" tall. Value: $45-85.

RONSON, c.1934. A "Gem" (L) and a "Princess" (R) lighter. Rhinestones and Chrome over brass. 2" tall. Value: $25-45.

RONSON, c.1934. Two De-light lighters. The larger lighter is Sterling silver and the smaller is a "Junior" in chrome. 2" and 1.75" tall. Value: (L-R) $125 to 225, $75-150.

RONSON, c.1934. The "Lincoln" striker model. The original sculpture was done by Gutzon Borglum in 1910 and sits in front of the Essex County, New Jersey, courthouse. The striker rod was hidden in Lincoln's hat and would be struck against the flint on the front left side. 6" tall. Value: $175-250.

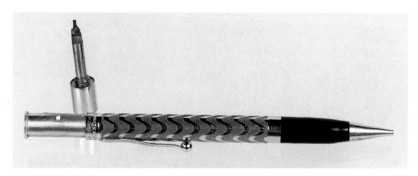

RONSON, c.1934. A chrome and plastic pencil striker lighter called the "Lite-O-Rite." 6" tall. Value: $250-350.

RONSON, c.1934. Two "New Yorker" model lighters. Bakelite plastic and chrome. 3" tall. Value: $200-250.

RONSON, c.1934. Two piece "Princess" set. Brown and white enamel with chrome highlights. 2" tall. Value: $125-175.

RONSON, c.1934. Two piece brown enamel "Princess" set. Brown enamel with chrome highlights. 2" tall. Value: $100-150.

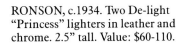

RONSON, c.1934. Sterling silver "Princess" lighters. Difficult to find in silver. 2" tall. Value: $150-200.

RONSON, c.1934. Two De-light "Princess" lighters in leather and chrome. 2.5" tall. Value: $60-110.

RONSON, c.1934. Two "Princess" lighters in two tone enamel and chrome. 2" tall. Value: $100-150.

RONSON, c.1934. A chrome "Baby Rondelight On Base" lighter. 4" tall. Value: $500-600.

RONSON, c.1934. "Regent Junior" lighters. Gold plate and Chrome with two tone enamel. 2.5" tall. Value: $60-100.

RONSON, c.1934. Two "Rondelight Ball" model lighters. Chrome and enamel. 3" tall. Value: $150-200.

RONSON, c.1934. A "Rondelight Junior" model leather-covered, ball-shaped lighter. Chrome and painted wood. 3" tall. Value: $100-150.

RONSON, c.1934. A "Rondelight Ball" lighter in the largest and hardest to find size. Chrome finish. 3.5" tall. Value: $200-300.

RONSON, c.1934. A "Rondette" table lighter. Chrome and enamel. 3.5" tall. Value: $150-200.

RONSON, c.1934. Examples of two different size lighters: a "Rondette" on the left and a "Rondette Junior" on the right. Chrome with brown enamel. Value: $55-100.

RONSON, c.1934. A "Rondette" lighter. Chrome with black enamel. 2.5" tall. Value: $60-80.

RONSON, c.1934. "Rondette Junior" lighters. Chrome with enamel. 2.5" tall. Value: $75-100.

RONSON, c.1934. "Standard" lighter. Enameled scene with a silver jacket. 2" tall. Value: $200-300.

RONSON, c.1934. (L) "Standard Twin Bar" lighter, first manufactured in 1929 and (R) "Standard Modernistic." Both were made with only one color of enamel. 2" tall. Value: $100-200.

RONSON, c.1934. De-light lighter made for Tiffany. The bottom is marked "Ronson De-light" and "Tiffany." 14kt gold. 2.5" tall. Value: $1,000-1,400.

RONSON, c.1934. "Standard" lighter in two tone enamel and chrome. 2" tall. Value: $100-150.

RONSON, c.1934. A chrome "Tube" or "Pipeliter" lighter with a pipe tamper at the other end. 5.5" tall. Value: $100-150.

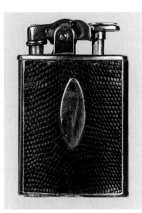

RONSON, c.1934. An unusual over-sized Ronson De-light lighter. Leather and nickel plate. 3" tall. Value: $65-100.

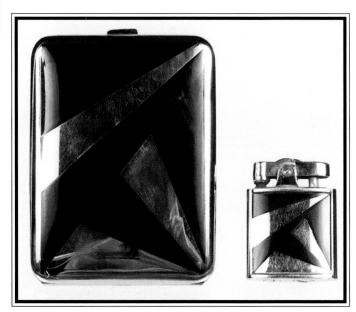

RONSON, c.1934. Two piece Deco set. Black enamel with chrome. 2" tall. Value: $100-200.

RONSON, c.1934. A De-light table lighter with a cameo. Chrome and black lacquer. 4" tall, 3" wide. Value: $200-300.

RONSON, c.1934. A chrome and plastic pencil lighter. 6" tall. Value: $30-40.

RONSON, c.1934. An unusual model lighter with a New Yorker fitment. Bakelite plastic and chrome. 3" tall. Value: $500-700.

RONSON, c.1934. An onyx lighter with a New Yorker fitment. Chrome and marble. 3" tall. Value: $250-350.

RONSON, c.1935. The Ronson Bartender Touch-tip is perhaps the most widely recognized Ronson lighter. It had cigarette compartments on the sides and was made of chrome plated and enameled brass. 7" tall, 6" wide. Value: $1500-2000.

RONSON, c.1935. A Touch-tip "Modernistic" lighter. Antique bronze finish on metal. Also available in a bright chrome finish. 4.5" tall. Value: $350-550.

RONSON, c.1935. "Regal" lighter. Chrome with black enamel. This is a very rare narrow model. 3" tall. Value: $400-600.

RONSON, c.1935. Two pre-war "Octette" Touch-tip table lighters. Chrome and enamel. Note the square metal cover over the flint wheel. Post-war models had curved housing. 4.5" tall. Value: $75-150.

RONSON, c.1935. A Touch-tip "Smoker's Set." Chrome and enamel. This set has a removable Octette Touch-tip between 2 cedar lined boxes. 4" tall. Value: $400-450.

RONSON, c.1935. A Ronson Touch-tip lighter with a clock. The clock is unusual as it has a pull winding system. When the cord was pulled, it would wind the clock. Chrome and enamel. 5.75" tall. Value: $700-1,200.

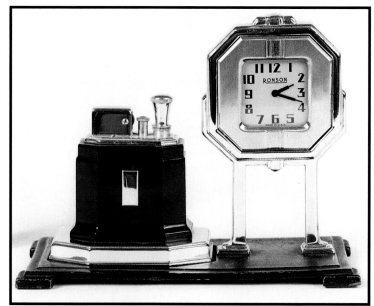

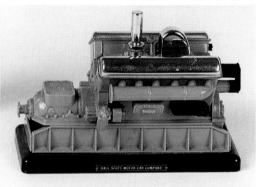

RONSON, c.1935. A Hall-Scott Motor Car Company table lighter. Plastic and chrome metal. Custom made for the Hall-Scott Company. A narrow tapered wand Touch-tip and very curved flint wheel cover. 6.5" tall. Value: $350-650.

RONSON, c.1936. A Golfer with a "Rondelight" lighter and ashtray. Chrome with a black gunmetal base. About 5.5" tall. Value: $700-1,200.

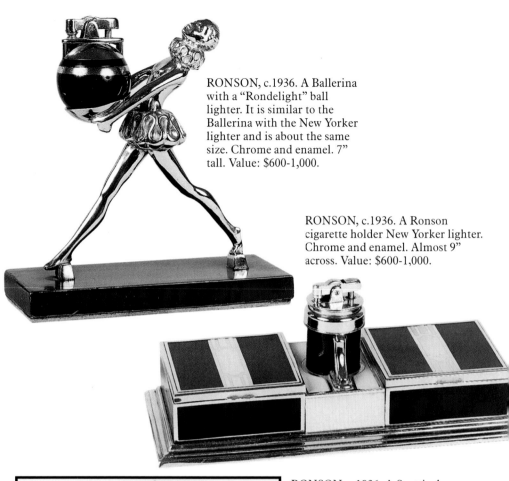

RONSON, c.1936. A Ballerina with a "Rondelight" ball lighter. It is similar to the Ballerina with the New Yorker lighter and is about the same size. Chrome and enamel. 7" tall. Value: $600-1,000.

RONSON, c.1936. A Ronson cigarette holder New Yorker lighter. Chrome and enamel. Almost 9" across. Value: $600-1,000.

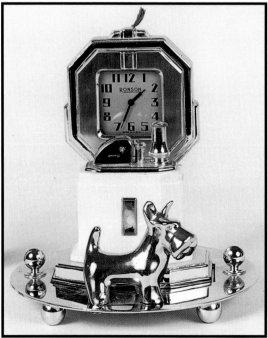

RONSON, c.1936. A Scottie dog, clock (with a pull winding mechanism visible and sitting on two stilts), Touch-tip "Octette" lighter. Chrome and enamel. 5.75" tall. Value: $1,500-2,000.

Opposite page
Top: RONSON, c.1936. A Touch-tip cigar humidor (with a removable lid) lighter. Chrome and enamel. 4.675" tall, 10" wide. Value: $850-1,250.

Center: RONSON, c.1936. Two clock Touch-tip lighters. These were introduced in 1936. Chrome and enamel, but also available in tortoise & chrome. Two size variations. Value: $350-550.

Bottom right: RONSON, c.1936. "The Diver" table lighter, one of several athletic theme lighters. The lighter is a "Baby Rondelight" ball in Chrome and enamel. About 5.5" tall. Value: $900-1,500.

RONSON, c.1936. A "Literpact" compact/lighter. The front opens and contains a powder puff, sifter, and mirror. These lighter/compact combinations are highly collectible. Dureum finish with green enamel and rhinestones. About 3.5" tall. Value: $150-250.

RONSON, c.1936. A Terrier dog with a New Yorker table lighter. Painted cast white metal. 5.75" tall. Value: $400-600.

RONSON, c.1936. The "Sleeping Man" with a New Yorker lighter. Painted metal. 5" tall. Value: $1,000-1,500.

RONSON, c.1936. Two "Streamline" Touch-tip table lighters with a nice Art Deco feel. Chrome and enamel. 3.75" tall. Value: $175-300.

RONSON, c.1936. A Touch-tip with ashtray table lighter. Gold plate and enamel. Identical to previous "Streamline" Touch-tips, but this sits on a matching base with an ashtray. 3.5" tall. Value: $800-1,200.

RONSON, c.1936. A Touch-tip with Roll-top cigarette cabinet lighter. Tortoise finish with chrome. 4" tall. Value: $550-850.

RONSON, c.1936. A Penguin New Yorker "Pik-a-cig" lighter and cigarette dispenser. A New Yorker fitment and a penguin that bobbed for cigarettes when the two levers beside the box were squeezed. Chrome and enamel. Also came in a hammered aluminum finish and as a striker model. 4.5" tall, 8" wide. Value: $700-1,100.

RONSON, c.1936. A Touch-tip "Classic" lighter. Missing the ashtrays. Black and chrome. 8.25" long. Value: $350-600.

RONSON, c.1936. A Touch-tip Roll Top Cabinet-Lighter. As the tray is pulled open, the chrome cover opens over the top level. Chrome and enamel. 8" wide x 6.25" deep. Value: $500-800.

RONSON, c.1936. A Touch-tip pipe holder lighter. Bronze finish with a tapered wand and curved flint wheel cover. 7.5" tall. Value: $300-500.

RONSON, c.1936. A Ronson Elephant table lighter with a New Yorker fitment. Painted metal with Ivoroid tusks. 6.5" tall. Value: $800-1,000.

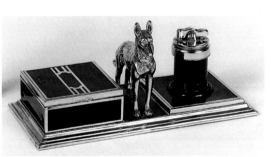

RONSON, c.1936. A Ronson New Yorker cigarette holder table lighter with a dog. Chrome and enamel. 9" wide. Value: $450-650.

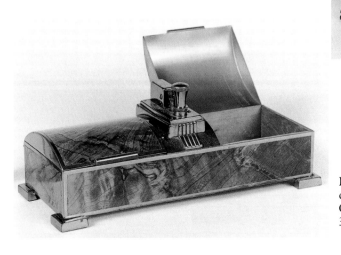

RONSON, c.1936. A Ronson Touch-tip with pipe rests. Antique bronze finish with curved flint wheel cover and narrow tapered Touch-tip wand. Value: $500-600.

RONSON, c.1936. A Touch-tip double cigarette holder lighter. Gold plated and faux bois finish. 3.5" tall. Value: $325-425.

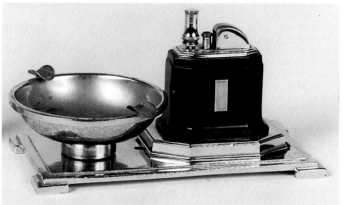

RONSON, c.1936. A Ronson Touch-tip with ashtray. An Octette lighter along side a large chrome ashtray. Chrome and enamel. Value: $400-500.

RONSON, c.1936. A Touch-tip Deluxe lighter. Tortoise lacquer semi-oval lighter on an oval base. 3.5" tall. Value: $200-300.

RONSON, c.1936. A Ronson "Earl." This is an extremely rare table lighter. Silver plated metal. 3" tall. Value: $500-900.

RONSON, c.1936. A "Chips" model lighter. It looks like a stack of poker chips. Chrome and enamel. 3.5" tall. Value: $300-500.

RONSON, c.1936. A "Decanter," first model lighter. Chrome finish. 3" tall. Value: $150-250.

RONSON, c.1937. A Ronson Touch-tip with an oval cigarette box. Introduced in 1937, along with another model with a single cigarette box on the right side. Gold plate and enamel. 8" long. Value: $350-500.

RONSON, c.1937. A very rare Ronson Touch-tip humidor with pipe rests. Similar to other Touch-tip models, but this one allows for the storage of tobacco inside. Gold plate and bronze finish. Value: $1,500-1,800.

RONSON, c.1937. A Touch-tip oval lighter, first model. Chrome and enamel. This model had the tapered wand and square flint wheel housing. The later version had a squared wand and a curved flint wheel housing. Value: $150-300.

RONSON, c.1937. A "Norseman Junior" Touch-tip table lighter. Silver plated with chrome insert and square pre-war flint cover. 4" tall. Value: $150-250.

RONSON, c.1937. A Touch-tip smoker's set cigarette holder and lighter. Chrome and enamel. 6" tall. Value: $1,000-1,500.

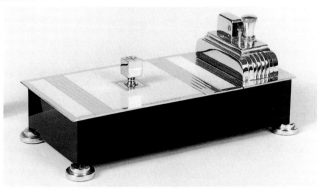

RONSON, c.1937. A Touch-tip and cigarette box lighter. Chrome and enamel. 3.25" tall, 8" wide. Value: $250-350.

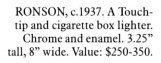

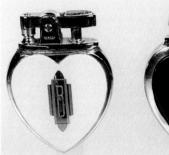

RONSON, c.1937. Heart lighters. Black or white enamel and chrome. 2.5" tall. Value: $250-450.

Right: RONSON, c.1938. A Ronson pipe holder Touch-tip lighter. Bronze finish on metal. Value: $250-450.

Below: RONSON, c.1937. A Touch-tip lighter with 8 day clock. Dureum on tortoise finish. The largest of the clock Touch-tips. 5" tall, 7" wide. Value: $850-1,250.

Above: RONSON, c.1937. Viceroy lighters. Gold plate and chrome with enamel. 2.5" tall. Value: $60-85.

Below: RONSON, c.1938. (L) Ronson "Standard Windbreak" and (R) "Princess Windbreak" lighters with windguards. Chrome finish. 2" tall. Value: $100-200.

RONSON, c.1938. A "Grecian" Touch-tip table lighter. Chrome and enamel. This is the later model with a tapered rod and curved flint housing. Originally sold for $5.00 in 1938. 4" tall. Value: $100-200.

RONSON, c.1938. A Touch-tip "Classic" lighter. Dureum finish with tortoise enamel. 4.5" tall. Value: $175-250.

RONSON, c.1938. A Touch-tip with cigarette box. Silver plated metal with a green Bakelite handle. 4" tall. Value: $1,200-1,600.

RONSON, c.1938. A Touch-tip "Classic" with ashtray. Dureum finish with tortoise lacquer. Originally had a glass ashtray. 3.5" tall. Value: $350-550.

RONSON, c.1938. A Ronson "Duette and China Tray Lighter." The lighter is removable and has a ribbed collar that sits directly in a china ashtray. 4" tall. Value: $400-600.

RONSON, c.1938. A "Decanter and Cigarette Tray" set. Plastic containers and silver plated metal. 5.25" deep x 14" wide. Value: $300-400. (The decanter alone is valued at $20-30.)

RONSON, c.1939. A Ronson Touch-tip cigarette dispenser table lighter. When the lever on the left is pushed, a cigarette rolls out. Chrome and enamel. 7.75" wide. Value: $350-550.

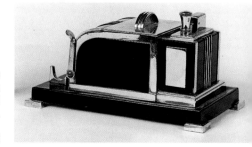

RONSON, c.1939. A Touch-tip and ash tray lighter. Gold plated metal. This model has a removable metal ashtray rather than the later glass ashtray. 5.5" tall. Value: $500-800.

RONSON, c.1939. A Touch-tip "Dynastic" lighter. Silver plated metal. 3.25" in diameter. Value: $250-350.

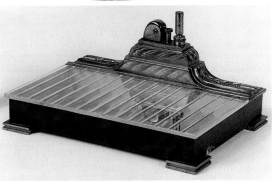

RONSON, c.1939. A Touch-tip with cigarette holder. The cover for the cigarettes is a form of plastic. Early curved flint wheel housing and tapered wand. Gold plated and enamel. 3.5" tall. Value: $400-600.

RONSON, c.1939. A Nautical Touch-tip lighter with a ship's wheel. Bronze and faux bois finish. 3.25" tall. Value: $175-275.

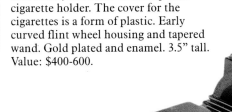

RONSON, c.1939. A "List Finder" telephone number table lighter. Antique bronze finish on gold plated metal. Also available in a striker lighter version. 4.75" deep x 9.5" wide. Value: $1,250-1,650.

RONSON, c.1939. A Touch-tip "Grecian Pipe" holder lighter. Bronze finish on metal. The lighter is removable. 7.25" base. Value: $350-600.

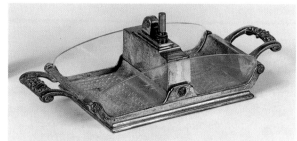

RONSON, c.1940. A Touch-tip and cigarette tray set. Glass and silver plated metal. 4.5" deep x 10.5" wide. Value: $600-900.

RONSON, c.1939. A handsome Art Deco "Elliptic" Touch-tip table lighter. The finish is called Georgian Bronze. Produced from 1939 to the mid-1940s. 3.25" tall. Value: $150-250.

RONSON, 1940s. A Ronson lighter display. Value: $225-350.

RONSON, c.1939. A pre-war Turret Touch-tip table lighter. Georgian Bronze and brushed gold finish. Cylindrical surrounded by four black panels. About 4" tall. Value: $200-250.

RONSON, c.1940. A "Colonnade" Touch-tip table lighter. Gold plated, crystal plastic pillars, and faux bois finish. 4.25" tall. Value: $275-475.

RONSON, c.1941. A Touch-tip ashtray lighter. Bronze finish on metal. Note the curved flint wheel cover and narrow tapered rod found only on a few models. Glass ashtray is missing. Value: $350-600.

RONSON, c.1944. A Standard black painted Ronson issued during World War II. Its box would have been marked "Wartime Model." 2.5" tall. Value: $50-75.

RONSON, c.1950. "Debonair" lighter. This model with the chrome with enamel is very rare. 2.5" tall. Value: $400-500.

RONSON, c.1950. A "Carousel" table lighter. Chrome and wood. The lighter is removable and sits in a wooden holder. Made in England. 2.75" diameter. Value: $75-100.

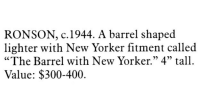

RONSON, 1950s-1960s. A great figural "Futura" lighter in the shape of a speedboat with a gas "Vara-flame" mechanism. 4" tall. Value: $40-80.

RONSON, c.1944. A barrel shaped lighter with New Yorker fitment called "The Barrel with New Yorker." 4" tall. Value: $300-400.

RONSON, c.1950. A chrome and plastic pencil lighter. 6" tall. Value: $20-30.

RONSON, c.1948. "RamaSpin" lighters. Ronson disguised its name, calling itself RAM (Ronson Art Metal). The RamaSpin was made to compete with the Zippo. It retailed for $2.95 at the time. Brown or black lacquer over zinc. 3" tall. Value: $40-80.

RONSON, c.1952. Two "Standard" lighters, one in gold and one in silver. 2.5" tall. Value: (L-R) $200-300, $100-175.

RONSON, c.1952 & 1964. "Minerva" model and a "Viola" model. 4" tall. Value: (L-R) $30-45, $25-35.

RONSON, c.1954 & 1936. Two table lighters. On the left is a "Savoy" in gold plate. The "Savoy" is similar to the "Decanter" but much rarer. On the right is the "Puritan." The "Puritan" is similar to the "Decanter" but much earlier. The "Puritan" was available in two versions. This is the later version with the beading on the top rim. 4.25" tall, 2" wide. Value: $100-200.

RONSON, c.1954. The "Adonis Smart Set." This chrome set came with cuff links and a tie clip. Its original was cost $20.00. 2" tall. Value: $75-150.

RONSON, c.1954. Two windproof lighters a "Typhoon" on the left and a "Windlite" on the right. They are unusual in that they carry advertising. 3" tall. Value: $50-100.

RONSON, c.1954. Two "Standard" lighters, one with advertising. These were produced from 1928 well into the 1950s. Chrome. 2.5" tall. Value: $25-75.

RONSON, c.1954. Two table lighters in silver plate. The "Regal" is on the left and the "Colonial" is on the right. 3.5" tall. Value: (L-R) $85-135, $35-50.

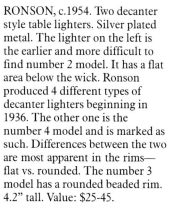

RONSON, c.1954. A "Kitchenette" table lighter with an "Essex" fitment which is harder to find. Decorated enamel finish. 4.5" tall. Value: $50-100.

RONSON, c.1954. Two decanter style table lighters. Silver plated metal. The lighter on the left is the earlier and more difficult to find number 2 model. It has a flat area below the wick. Ronson produced 4 different types of decanter lighters beginning in 1936. The other one is the number 4 model and is marked as such. Differences between the two are most apparent in the rims—flat vs. rounded. The number 3 model has a rounded beaded rim. 4.2" tall. Value: $25-45.

RONSON, c.1954. Two "Jumbo" chrome plated lighters. 4.5" tall. Value: $100-150.

RONSON, c.1955. Three "Senator" table lighters with leather and cloth covering. 3.5" tall. Value: $20-45.

RONSON, c.1956. A Ronson "Spartan" table lighter. Chrome and enamel. 3" wide. Value: $40-80.

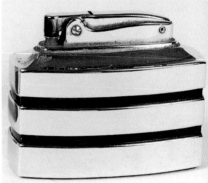

RONSON, c.1955. Chromium "Tempo" model lighter. 4" tall. Value: $35-45.

RONSON, c.1958. Two "Leona" table lighters. 3.5" tall. Value: $25-40.

RONSON, c.1958. Two table lighters, one in silver plate and the other with a copper finish. A "Juno" on the left and a "Colony" on the right. 7" and 3.5" tall. Value: (L-R) $30-60, $20-40.

RONSON, c.1958. Two table lighters. A "Tempo" on the left and a "Newport" on the right. 3.5" tall. Value: (L-R) $25-45, $20-35.

RONSON, c.1959. An English "Cadet" model lighter. Transfer decorated china. 3" tall. Value: $100-150.

RONSON, c.1959. The Ronson "Decor" was a futuristic lighter in the shape of a flying saucer. These were sold clear and the owner could insert a piece of fabric matching the decor of the room. These used lighter fluid. 3" tall, 4" wide. Value: $25-40.

RONSON, c.1959. Two table lighters. A "Tempo" on the left and a "Trophy" on the right. 3.5" tall. Value: (L-R) $30-40, $25-45.

RONSON, c.1962. Three "Minton China Co." lighters. Transfer decorated china. 3" tall. Value: $150-200.

RONSON, c.1964. Two table lighters by Wedgewood. The "Four Seasons" is on the left and the "Royalty" is on the right. 3.5" tall. Value: $35-65.

ROYDEN, c.1935. The perfect lighter for the lady's purse. It is very compact and fits into a tube thinner than a lipstick case. The top comes off to expose a simple flint and wheel lighter and the bottom comes off to release a collapsible cigarette holder. 3" tall. Value: $50-100.

RONSON, c.1978. The Ronson "Varachem Penliter" was made by Ronson of England. It used a Varachem cartridge for an electronic spark so it did not use flints. Value: $40-70.

SAM, c.1935. A French lighter in 18kt gold. Note the small ring on the side so that it could be attached to a chain to prevent it from being lost. 2.5" tall. Value: $1,000-1,300.

SARACTO, c.1955. A Sterling silver lighter with a watch in its side. 2.5" tall. Value: $500-700.

SCRIPTO: 1950s to 1980

This Atlanta, Georgia, company made the VU-Lighter with a see-through body. They have become more popular in the last few years and are rising in price. Most people are familiar with the lighter containing the fishing fly, their most popular model. Unusual models are turning up. They can be found in great variety and their price range is, for the most part, reasonable. As with Zippo, salesman's samples and the advertising models are more desirable—and, the more unusual, the better.

Scriptos can be found showing bowlers, fisherman, hunters, baseball players, golfers, trout, sailfish, sea shells, a seahorse, dice, religious medal, and advertising inserts. The fishing fly was included in lighters made from the late 1950s to about 1980. The earlier flies were usually one or two colors; the later flies were up to four colors with the major color matching the plastic of the lighter.

Cleaning Scripto lighters

Very often, a collector will come across a Scripto that has so much discoloration inside the fuel tank that they can not see what is inside. The tank can be cleaned out and made to look much better. Try cotton swabs on wooden sticks.

SCRIPTO, c.1958. Four compact model Scripto VU-lighters with black or blue bands and various designs inside. Value: $30-40.

SCRIPTO, c.1958. A rare Scripto VU-lighter with the well-known (on the east coast) White Castle hamburger store inside. At the time, these small hamburgers were 12 cents each. Yummmm! Let's eat twenty. Value: $75-150.

SCRIPTO, c.1958. Four Scripto VU-lighters with black or blue bands and outdoor sports theme designs inside. Value: $25-45.

SCRIPTO, c.1958. Two Scripto VU-lighters with black bands and fishing and hunting theme designs inside. Value: $25-45.

SCRIPTO, c.1959. A pair of Scripto VU-lighter with Scripto advertising. These are acknowledged as having been given to Scripto salesmen to use and show as examples. Value: $100-150.

SCRIPTO, c.1958. An assortment of Scripto VU-lighters with a variety of inserts. The most desirable is the "Pin up girl" model. 3" tall. Value: $25-60.

SCRIPTO, c.1960. Three VU-lighter lighters with the Pepsi-Cola being the most valuable. The lavender "I'm a Pussycat" is the most unusual color. 2.5" tall. Value: $50-125 (w/box).

SCRIPTO, c.1958. A great VU-Lighter table lighter with a pink poodle. 3.5" tall. Value: $100-150.

SCRIPTO, c.1960. A close-up of the VU-lighter with an ad insert for Pepsi-Cola. Value: $75-125.

SCRIPTO, c.1960. A close-up of the VU-lighter with a "I am a Pussycat" insert. Value: $50-80.

SCRIPTO, c.1960. A VU-lighter with a black band and an interesting electrical diagram inside. Value: $40-75.

SCRIPTO, c.1960. Three different VU-lighters with Sports themes. A duck for the hunter, a bowler, and a golfer graced the inside of these lighters. Value: $30-45.

SCRIPTO, c.1960. Three different Scripto "Goldenglo" VU-lighters with gold plated metal parts. These are the "compact" size and included designs and a butterfly inside. Value: $25-35.

SCRIPTO, c.1960. Table model VU-Lighter lighters. 4" tall. Value: $50-75.

SCRIPTO, c.1960. An very odd VU-lighter with a hypodermic needle inside. It is so odd as to be suspect, but the needle is so long and wide that the lighter had to have been assembled with it inside. Could it possibly have been made by an employee for the company doctor? Value: $75-125.

SCRIPTO, c.1962. An Advertising VU-lighter with a red band and a robot-like character inside. Value: $50-75.

SCRIPTO, c.1961. An unusual VU-lighter with a red band and a compass inside. Also shown is its original paper box. Value: $50-90 (w/box).

SCRIPTO, c.1962. A VU-lighter with a turquoise blue band and a fishhook inside. Note that the fluid reservoir is also a blue color on this model. Value: $40-80.

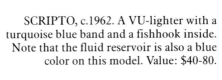

SCRIPTO, c.1962. An unusual Marlboro advertising VU-lighter in its original tin box. Made in Atlanta, Georgia. Value: $75-150.

SCRIPTO, c.1964. A VU-lighter with the Star of Israel. Value: $40-80.

SCRIPTO, c.1962. A Table VU-lighter with its original box. The lighter contains an Allstate Insurance Co. ad insert. Value: $75-125.

SCRIPTO, c.1962. A mint condition VU-lighter with a sparkle pattern insert. It has a rare colored tank body. Value: $40-75.

SCRIPTO, c.1964. A mint VU-lighter with a golfer insert and a red band. Value: $50-80.

135

SCRIPTO, c.1964. A mint, rare VU-lighter advertising VU-lighters. Value: $75-125.

SCRIPTO, c.1966. A compact VU-lighter with a black band and a Coca-Cola advertisement inside. As with Zippo lighters, the value increases with unusual or major company advertising. Value: $100-150.

SCRIPTO, c.1964. A VU-lighter called the "Goldenglo" containing an advertising insert for Snowy Bleach and Mr. Bubble bubble bath with an unusual pink band. Value: $40-80.

SCRIPTO, c.1968. A pocket VU-lighter with its original box. The lighter contains a psychedelic optical art design insert. Value: $40-80.

SCRIPTO, c.1968. Two "psychedelic" Scripto "VU-lighters" in their original boxes. 3" tall. Value: $50-100.

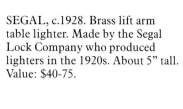

SCRIPTO, c.1980. This appears to be a 1962 era Scripto, but our Scripto expert identifies it as a 1980s lighter with a stock Scripto base and non-Scripto chimney. Value: $30-45.

SILEX, c.1945. A Swiss made lighter with a classic mechanism in chrome-plated metal. Value: $75-100.

SILENT FLAME, c.1935. An ashtray, clock, and electric lighter set in wood. 3" tall. Value: $150-200.

STELLA-VEGA, c.1938. An unusual French made, silver plated lighter with a mechanism that drops down when the lighter is closed and rises up when it is opened. Value: $250-300.

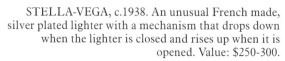

STRIKE-A-LITE, c.1955. Three colorful American lighters made to resemble perfume bottles. 3" tall. Value: $20-40.

SUNBEAM, c.1935. An electric lighter, ashtray, and cigarette dispenser. The cigarette was dispensed lit. 3" tall. Value: $250-350.

STURDY, c.1932. A chrome plated flip top U.S. made lighter. Value: $75-100.

SWANK, c.1960. A Japanese television shaped lighter. When the antenna is pushed down, the lighter lights. The TV is also a working slide viewer. It is difficult to find with the antenna intact. 6" tall. Value: $60-90.

SWANK, c.1928. The "Kum-A-Part" lighter. Chrome plate with enamel. This has great early Art Deco styling. Value: $200-250.

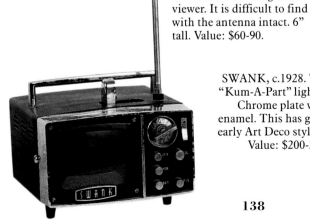

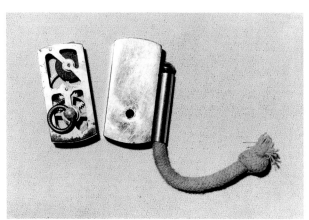

SWANK, c.1964. A sports car with a lighter built into the roof. Made in Japan, it used petrol as a fuel. 5.5" long. Value: $85-125.

SYSTEM VAUDAINE, c.1880. A rope lighter patented in 1881 by Joseph Vaudaine with a mechanical striking mechanism. A hardy turn of the winding wheel would rub steel against flint to create a spark that would cause the rope to burn. Value: $350-450.

SWEETHEART, c.1953. A store display for "Sweetheart" lighters. A lady's little lighter and/or perfume container. The lighter slipped into the blue plastic heart. Value: $25-40 (individually).

THORENS, c.1921 & 1923. Two Thorens semi-automatic table models in onyx. The lighter on the left, with the exposed flint wheel, is earlier. Thorens were Swiss made (1920s to 1960s) and of the highest quality. Thorens was a music box maker that started in 1883. Their most sought after models are of the 1920s to 1930s era which include round models and watch lighters. The company moved into making record turntables, speakers, and other music items. 4.5" tall. Value: (L-R) $50-75, $35-55.

TANDEM, c.1946. The Tandem was an aluminum lighter with 2 flint wheels, two flint tubes, and two wicks. This one was made in Poland, but other similar versions have been found that were made in England and Austria. Value: $100-200.

THORENS, c.1922. Thorens lighters are great mechanical items. They were so well made that with a bit of cleaning almost all of them can be made to work. The model on the left has an unusual round shape. The model on the right is the standard shape. Value: (L-R) $175-225, $30-50.

THORENS, c.1922. A chrome plated cigar lighter with a semi-automatic action and its original box. The earlier Thorens had a cut away area to access the friction wheel (single claw model). In later models the case was straight across. Value: $75-150.

THORENS, c.1925. A small sized Thorens automatic lighter with a watch in its side. 2.5" tall. Value: $1,000-1,400.

THORENS, c.1925. Two Sterling silver Thorens automatic lighters. Note the two different locations of filling screw, one on the side and one on the bottom. 2.5" and 2.75" tall. Value: $350-450 ea.

THORENS, c.1932. A rare pipe lighting model called the "Teleflam." This Swiss made lighter has a nice design feature. The wheel on the side extends the wick tube, once it is lit, making it easier to light a pipe. Value: $400-500.

Tinder, c.1930. A grouping of tinder style lighters. These operated without fuel. The tinder rope just smoldered. Excellent for use in high winds and lighting numerous smokes at a time. Value: $20-40.

THORENS, c.1940. A very rare Thorens lighter. This was called the "Blizzard" and was only made for a few years. Chrome metal. 2.75" tall. Value: $400-500.

TIPS, c.1933. A pair of interesting European lighters. The lighter on the left had an arm to push down upon to operate, while the one on the right used a push button. Both were semi-automatic lighters. Value: $50-75.

TOP HAT, c.1937. A U.S. made lighter with its original box. Its safety feature was that you had to push the buttons on the front and back to make it operate. Chrome plated with a nice design to grip with slippery fingers. Value: $125-150.

TOMMY, c.1934. The Tommy "Pipelighter" with tamper in chrome metal (model also available without the tamper). Made in England. Value: $60-90.

141

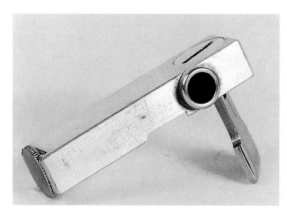

TRANSFO, c.1941. A French made lighter that used no fuel. The cigarette was placed inside the opening and the handle was turned creating enough of a spark to light the cigarette. The handle is flush to the body when not in use. Value: $75-125.

Trench Art, c.1918. Two nice trench art lighters from the first World War. A book style and a Kaiser Wilhelm model. Value: $75-150.

Trench Art, c.1918. An interesting trench art style lighter with a nude lady on both sides. Value: $50-100.

Trench Art, c.1918. This is a match safe in the shape of the German Crown Prince. Value: $150-200.

Trench Art, A group of W.W.I and W.W.II era trench art lighters. These are French and English and the flint wheel unscrews for refueling. Value: $50-100.

UNITY, c.1934. A beautifully enameled cigarette case and lighter. Sterling silver. Made in England. Value: $400-500.

Unknown, c.1908. A Sterling silver catalytic lighter. It used a special denatured alcohol that reacted with air and the tiny platinum balls to produce a flame. 2.75" tall. Value: $150-200.

Unknown, c.1900. A pair of flint and steel lighters. The spark would cause the rope to smolder so cigars and such could be lit from the burning rope. These have a clip at the end to snuff the burning rope. Value: $150-250.

Unknown, c.1900. A French figural match safe. Value: $100-130.

143

Unknown, 1910s. A nice selection of flask shaped, small striker lighters. The top loaded rod made contact with the fluid reservoir and was struck against the flint strip on the side or bottom. Value: $25-50.

Unknown, c.1912. A German made table lighter with a bronze bird base. One of a series of people and animals. Value: $45-75.

Unknown, c.1918. A shell lighter with no name. It was made in France and has the French tax stamp, marked Minister of Finance, around the lighter's body. Probably a post-war souvenir. Value: $25-50.

Unknown, c.1912. This is probably a European made automatic lighter but could be English made since it has a coronation plaque on the front. Value: $200-250.

Unknown, c.1920. Rebecca stands next to two Austrian made figural striker lighters. These could easily be overlooked when you are searching for lighters. The striker is hidden. Value: $300-400 ea.

Unknown, c.1920. A combination whistle and cigarette lighter in silver metal. About 3" long. Value: $150-250.

Unknown, c.1920. A bear in a tree tinder table lighter. The spark would start the tinder smoldering. No fuel was used, only flint. Value: $75-150.

Unknown, c.1922. A wonderful Austrian terrier dog lighter in pot metal. When you pulled back his head, the lighter lit. Value: $75-150.

Unknown, 1920s. An unusual Austrian hat shaped lighter. The top of the hat is shown off exposing the simple wheel, flint, and wick of the lighter. Value: $100-175.

Unknown, 1920s. A grouping of Bakelite lighters. All are unmarked but made in the U.S. The entire body is Bakelite and the top and filler screws are chrome. Value: $50-100.

Unknown, c.1922. A silver plated, English made striker lighter with ribbed design. It resembles a match safe and might be overlooked by the lighter collector. The striker strip is on the bottom. Value: $150-200.

Unknown, c.1924 A bear shaped striker lighter in nickel plated metal. It is possible that it was part of a smoke stand set. About 2.5" long. Value: $100-150.

Unknown, c.1925. An early French made lighter with a tax stamp that opened somewhat like a compact. The flint and wheel were mounted on the top and it used woven tinder. About 2" x 3". Value: $200-250.

Unknown, c.1925. A Sterling silver lift arm lighter with a windguard. Value: $75-150.

Unknown, c.1925. This English Sterling silver lighter used an unusual side hinged lid. 2.5" tall. Value: $300-400.

Unknown, c.1928. A golf ball shaped lighter in Sterling silver. It is engraved "2nd prize 1928 Golf tournament." About 3.5" tall. Sold by Udall & Ballou. Value: $450-500.

Unknown, c.1928. A French made hammered finish Sterling silver stand lighter. It has a simple friction wheel and a capped wick. 5" tall. Value: $80-120.

Unknown, 1920s to 1930s. An assortment of Bakelite plastic lift arm lighters. All are American made. 2.5" tall. All have similar values. Value: $30-65.

Unknown, c.1928. A chrome plated European lift arm lighter on a base. 7" tall. Value: $75-150.

Unknown, c.1928. Two examples of combination lighter/mechanical pencils. They are interesting in that the hole on the cap would have held a flint. When the cap was removed and struck against the friction area on the top of the clip, it would spark and light the wick. Early plastic over brass. Value: $40-75.

Unknown, c.1930. An elegant 18kt gold, French made lighter with sapphires set into the top of the cap. Value: $1,200-1,500.

Unknown, c.1929. An enameled lighter with a Venice, Italy, scene. It is similar to a Ronson De-light but has a much higher plunger. Value: $100-150.

Unknown, c.1932. A French lighter with an oriental motif. It has a hinged wick cover and the tax stamp is on the area where the dark portion meets the nickel plated part. About 3.5" tall. Value: $100-150.

Unknown, c.1933. A figural camel shaped lift arm lighter made in the United States. 4" tall. Value: $65-85.

Unknown, c.1930. A wolf in cowboy gear lighter. This unusual U.S. made striker lighter had its striker rod located in the base. You would then light up the area between the wolf's legs and pass him around to light cigarettes and cigars. Probably made for use in a men's club. There is a second variation that has the wick in the wolf's mouth. 5" tall. Value: $100-140.

Unknown, c.1934. An English made dog house striker lighter. The wand is in the back and the flint strip is in the front. Value: $175-250.

Unknown, c.1935. A French jerri-can style petrol lighter. The fluid screw is on the top right. Chrome plated sturdy brass. Value: $150-250.

Unknown, c.1935. A Sterling silver automatic lighter with a rare heart shaped windguard. 2.5" tall. Value: $200-300.

Unknown, c.1935. A jeweler made cigarette case with a built-in lighter. Sterling silver with an engine turned finish. Made in England and hallmarked Birmingham. Value: $300-400.

Unknown, c.1935. An enamel on Sterling silver English made lighter. 2.75" tall. Value: $450-550.

Unknown, c.1936. A beautiful Art Deco table striker lighter. Both sides are shown. This French made lighter is black enamel on Sterling silver. 3.75" tall. Value: $800-1,000.

Unknown, c.1936. This is an English made Champagne bottle and glasses striker table lighter in chrome plated brass. The "cork" of the bottle is attached to the striker rod. A flint strip located at the front of the base. 6" tall. Value: $100-200.

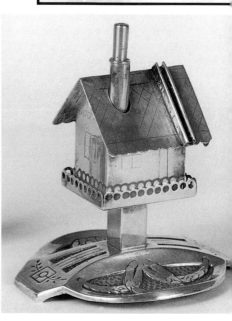

Unknown, c.1936. An French made striker style table lighter in the shape of a bird feeder. The wand is located on top on the roof along side the flint strip. Silver. Value: $350-500.

Unknown, c.1936. German table lighter with a pull chain to activate mechanism. About 6" tall. Value: $75-125.

Unknown, c.1936. On first glance you would swear that this is a typical Ronson Touch-tip lighter. It is a copy and could have been made in Japan. There are no markings. Value: $100-150.

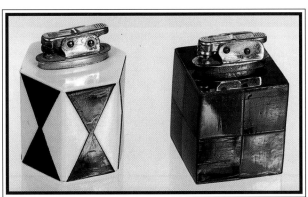

Unknown, c.1936. An Art Deco lighter that was made in France. About 4" tall. Value: $125-200.

Unknown, c.1936. A pair of Bakelite or plastic lighters that were made in Japan. About 2.5" tall. Value: $100-125.

Unknown, c.1936. A Bakelite or plastic lighter in the shape of a car that was made in England. The trunk or boot pulls out to access the lighter. About 3" long. Value: $225-275.

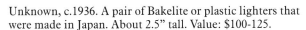

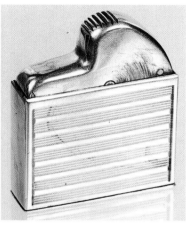

Unknown, c.1937. A (900) silver, German made lighter with an interesting design. Value: $125-175.

Unknown, c.1938. A two piece set of electric table lighter and cigarette holder. Value: $100-200.

Unknown, c.1938. A U.S. made golf theme lighter. To activate it, one would push down on the golf club. About 5.5" tall. Value: $150-200.

Center left: Unknown, c.1938. A nice butterscotch colored Bakelite striker lighter. The flint strip is on the bottom. About 3" tall. Value: $100-150.

Bottom left: Unknown, c.1940. An English table lighter in the shape of a sundial. The sundial, attached to a rod, pulls out and strikes against the base. Value: $100-150.

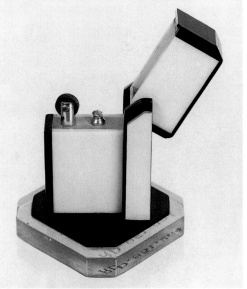

Unknown, c.1940. A pair of very unusual looking plastic lighters with hinged lids. Both were probably made in England. The red one is about 4" tall and the white and black one is about 3" tall. Value: $125-200.

Unknown, c.1940. An attractive German lamp post lighter. Pulling the chain produced the flame. 7" tall. Value: $20-40.

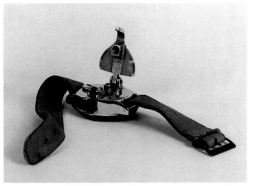

Unknown, 1940s. An unusual Chinese made gun shaped lighter. The complex looking action is chrome plated brass. 4" long. Value: $200-300.

Unknown, 1940s. An unusual watch shaped lighter. The snuffer is in the up position. Made in England. Value: $400-600.

Unknown, 1945. A small Japanese lighter that is engraved "Xmas 1945" and the name of a hospital in Japan. The flame came out the top and the holes are the wind screen. Value: $40-80.

Unknown, c.1944. An aluminum handmade lighter, ashtray, and cigarette case in the shape of a mosque. The lighter is inside the tower on the left. This was probably made in North Africa using aircraft aluminum. Value: $125-225.

Unknown, c.1945. A by-product of the Second World War was a surplus of aluminum. Some European craftsman made this table lighter from aluminum and decorated it with a nude. 4" tall. Value: $100-200.

Unknown, c.1945. A mortar and pestle and ashtray made in the United States. The perfect gift for the local pharmacist. The pestle opened to expose the simple flint and wheel lighter. 2.5" tall. Value: $40-70.

Unknown, c.1946. Two aluminum table lighters with two wicks made in Italy. The extra wick is at the end of the rod. The rod unscrewed and the wick at the end was lit and used for a pipe or passed around. 4" tall. Value: $75-125.

Unknown, c.1947. A figural elephant shaped lighter made in Japan. 4" tall. Value: $25-50.

Above: Unknown, c.1948. An interesting double wheeled lighter. When the wheel is turned, the arm pops up. When closed, it resembles a small (5-inch) cocktail shaker. Made in Germany. Value: $150-200.

Right: Unknown, c.1948. Metal lighter in the shape of the Johnson Wax Tower in Racine, Wisconsin, a building designed by Frank Lloyd Wright. There were 5000 of these made. Collected by building collectors also. About 6.5" tall. Value: $300-450.

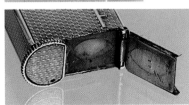

Unknown, c.1947. A French made lighter in Sterling silver. It has an unusual filling system. The large screw is turned and the bottom pops open to fill. Value: $250-300.

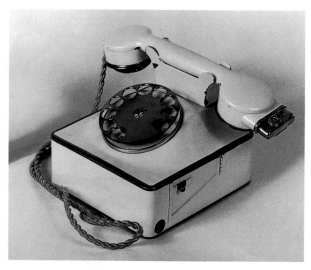

Unknown, c.1950. A telephone shaped cigarette dispenser and lighter. It was made in Germany and was all metal with the lighter in the handset and a music box inside. Value: $100-200.

Unknown, c.1952. White metal lighter made in Japan. 7" tall. Value: $30-40.

Unknown, c.1950. A novelty snake-in-the-can lighter made in Japan. When the lever is pushed down, the snake comes flying out of the spot where the flame would be. A great gift for those trying to quit smoking. Value: $15-20.

Unknown, c.1953. A wonderful Sunoco gasoline pump with a lighter inside. 3.75" tall. Value: $200-300.

Unknown, c.1953. Novelty soda and beer can lighters with fitments made in Japan. 6" tall. Value: $20-40.

Unknown, c.1953. Novelty beer can lighters with fitments made in Japan. 6" tall. Value: $20-40.

Unknown, c.1953. A Japanese pedestal lighter with two nude cherubs. 5" tall. Value: $25-40.

Unknown, c.1953. A group of knights in armor. Each knight has a different mechanism, but they are all contained in the knight's head. Some are automatic and some are manual. The second from the left has a musical base. 8" to 10" tall. Value: $50-100.

Unknown, c.1953. A novelty Japanese table lighter in the shape of a pink elephant. 6" tall. Value: $20-30.

Unknown, 1950s. A Japanese Zippo type lighter with an unusual black Mickey Mouse. Value: $40-80.

Unknown, 1950s. A pair of Italian decorated silver cased lighters that would have taken a Zippo lighter insert (standard and slim). Value depends upon the quality, subject matter, and execution of the artwork. Value: $75-175.

Unknown, 1950 to 1960s. A small group of car lighters made in Japan. 3" tall. Value: $25-35.

Unknown, c.1955. Two ships wheel design table lighters in a chrome plated metal. The larger lighter has a music box in the base and both operate the lighter by turning the wheel. Value: $25-55.

Unknown, c.1955. A musical lighter resembling a radio made in Japan. Pushing the white button activated the music and the lighter. 4" tall. Value: $60-80.

Unknown, c.1957. A pair of lighters with pin-up girl designs. Made in Japan. 2.5" tall. Value: $25-40.

Unknown, c.1958. A nice Zippo-type lighter with advertising for a plaster company. Value: $20-30.

Unknown, c.1958. A pair of Japanese novelty lighters. Roulette on the left and a perpetual calendar on the right. Value: $20-40.

Unknown, c.1960. A Japanese novelty lighter. Value depends upon the subject matter and quality of the work. This has a pretty Japanese scene. Value: $15-20.

Unknown, c.1960. A Japanese telephone shaped lighter with a built-in radio. The lighter is located on the handset. 6" tall. Value: $50-80.

Unknown, c.1960. A Japanese phonograph shaped lighter. When the needle is placed on the record, the turntable turns and plays music. 6" tall. Value: $60-90.

Unknown, c.1960. Two Japanese piano shaped lighters. Both operate by pushing down on the keyboard. 3" tall. Value: $50-90.

Unknown, c.1964. Three petrol chrome and enamel lighters made in Japan. 4" tall. Value: $5-15.

Unknown, c.1960. A great looking Japanese pipe lighter with a Modern Art black face design. Value: $60-90.

Unknown, c.1962. Julie holds a rocket shaped lighter. The chrome rocket is removable from the fins and it has a simple wheel and wick type lighter on the other end. About 7.5" tall. Value: $40-60.

Unknown, c.1964.
A pot metal lighter
in the shape of a
Kiwi bird. This
very attractive
lighter is perfect to
put in your guest
room when
expecting a visit
from your
Australian friends.
Value: $20-30.

Unknown, c.1964. A nice
Japanese musical lighter
made to sell during the
American Civil War
Centennial celebration.
Value: $40-75.

Unknown, c.1965. A pair of
decorated lighters, one with
riding cowboys and the other
with a Coca-Cola advertisement.
2.75" tall. Value: (L-R$) $100-
125, $150-200.

Unknown, c.1965. A stock
ticker lighter. This is a very
detailed lighter that even
has tape. When a button
under the glass is pushed,
the lighter on top lights.
Value: $60-90.

Unknown, c.1970. A
Japanese slot machine
shaped butane lighter.
When the arm is pulled, the
three wheels inside turn. 5"
tall. Value: $30-60.

VICEROY, c.1925. A tall 9kt gold, English made pocket lighter with a checkered design. Value: $400-500.

Unknown, c.1989. An attack helicopter lighter. Made in Japan. 3" tall. Value: $25-35.

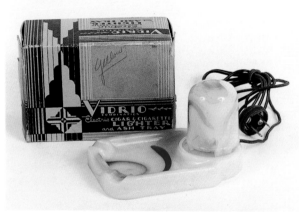

VIDRIO, c.1942. The American made Vidrio lighter/ashtray plugged into a wall socket. When the lighter was picked up, the coil on the bottom would heat up and glow. We wonder at the number of fires started by this nicely Deco designed, but poorly conceived, item. 3.5" tall. Value: $70-95 w/box.

WINDY, c.1939. An Austrian lighter similar in style to the Ronson "Vee." It h an Art Deco styled butterfly and include tassel. Value: $100-150.

ZENITH, c.1940. A German made lighter with an unusual feature—the front panel comes off to access the flint and fuel. Value: $50-75.

WIT, c.1929. A wall mounted lighter made in France. To light it, you would pass the wand, attached to the black handle, through the metal grate which would produce the sparks. 3" tall. Value: $125-170.

ZIPPO: 1932 to present

Here are a few words from the Zippo Museum Curator/archivist, Linda Meabon.

New collectors and seasoned veterans alike will find pleasure in collecting vintage lighters. Zippo lighters are like windows into time; company logos from the 1930s, WWII designs, and US Space mission commemoratives are all snapshots from different eras. Since 1933, almost 350 million Zippos lighters have been produced, recording nearly seven decades of history, one square-inch at a time. As evidenced by this book, thousands of people throughout the world find lighter collecting satisfying and fun. Some search for the elusive 1933 Zippos, while others try to piece together a comprehensive Vietnam collection. Through it all there remains a common bond between collectors. It is the thrill of the hunt, and the satisfaction of a rare find. Extraordinary lighters can be found in the strangest of places—in a garage sale, at a swap meet, perhaps even in your own basement. Once you start collecting, it may be a hard habit to break. (To learn more about Zippo products or starting a lighter collection, visit our website at www.zippo.com)

Zippo lighters almost all use the same mechanism. Zippo collectors collect social history. The lighters advertised or presented products or things, many that only existed for a short period of time. They reflect what happened during the years since the 1930s. Soldiers liked them and have used them in all the wars since the Second World War. Lighters were available in custom designs in lots as small as 50 pieces so that many groups could memorialize their achievements. Zippos were reliable and came with the best guarantee—if it breaks, Zippo will fix it for free!

One of the most beautiful models was the Town and Country made from 1949 to the 1960s with a few examples being made into the early 1970s. The Town and Countrys had a colorful handpainted or airbrushed design done over an etched or engraved surface. The roughed up surface helped hold the finish to the lighter. The brilliant colors were obtained using a material called Della Robba glaze. This glaze was applied one color at a time, and allowed to dry between the addition of each color/coat. Finally, the finished lighter was baked to cure and harden the glaze. Jack Clark, a Zippo Art director, should receive credit for the Town and Country idea. He was personally involved in producing the first models. The first commercial designs were animals—a mallard duck, a horse, an Irish setter, geese, a pheasant, and a trout—along with a sailing sloop and a water scene with a lily pad. A sailfish was added in the early 1950s. Not all colorful painted Zippos are Town and Country models. Zippo made most of its colorfully decorated lighters using a silkscreen method. The silkscreen method was quick and could be applied by skilled workers while the Town and Country finish was slow and required a greater artistic skill to produce the desired effect.

The Zippo Rule

In valuing Zippo advertising lighters, the most desirable lighters advertise Zippo or mention The Zippo Company.

The next most valuable category is lighters that advertise major companies that are no longer around such as De Soto cars, some cigarette companies, or defunct airlines.

Third are lighters that advertise and/or illustrate products that are no longer made such as typewriters, old televisions, old cars, famous restaurants no longer in business, etc.

Next in value are major companies—old logos, and then newer logos.

Next are local companies and local services.

Dating Zippo Lighters

1932—First model created by George Blaisdell. It is about one quarter inch longer than later models. It may actually have been made in early 1933.

1933 to 1935—The hinge connecting the top and bottom of the lighter case is soldered onto the outside of the case. The hinge is made up of 3 barrels: one center, usually connected to the bottom hinge plate and 2 outside, connected to the top hinge plate. The bottom of the lighter case is flat and the edges are squared off. The windscreen has 16 holes and the cap pressure bar pivot pin area is a part of the windscreen.

1936—The hinge is still soldered onto the outside of the case and is made up of 4 barrels. The bottom of the lighter case is still flat and the edges are squared off.

Mid to late 1936 to 1943—The hinge is now soldered on the inside of the case and is made up of 4 barrels. The bottom of the lighter case is still flat and the edges are squared off or rounded. 1937 is the beginning of the brass drawn case with a more rounded top and bottom. Formerly, the top was flat and soldered into place.

1943-1945—The hinge is made up of 3 barrels. The bottom of the lighter case is slightly rounded along with the edges.

1946-1950—The bottom of the lighter case is changed. It has a concave framed look; that is, there is an indented area where the imprint is located and the edges are rounded. In 1946, the windscreen is made with 14 holes. In 1947, the windscreen is made with 16 holes, and the metal supporting the wheel now connects to the top of the windscreen. The words ZIPPOMFG, on the inside unit, have no space between ZIPPO and MFG.

1951 forward—The hinge is made with 5 barrels.

1953 forward—The patent number is changed from 2032695 to 2517191.

1957 forward—There is now a code for year of manufacture on the bottom of the case (see illustration).

Charts produced by ZIPPO to aid in the identifaction of their lighters.

ZIPPO LIGHTER IDENTIFICATION CODES

YEAR	REGULAR		SLIM	
	LEFT	RIGHT	LEFT	RIGHT
1932	Patent Pending			
1937	Patent 2032695 *			
1950	Patent 2517191			
1957	Full stamp with patent pending		••••	••••
1958	Full stamp, no patent pending			
	••••	••••	•••	•••
1959	••••	•••	•••	•••
1960	•••	•••	•••	•••
1961	•••	••	••	••
1962	••	••	••	•
1963	••	•	•	•
1964	•	•	•	
1965	•			
1966	IIII	IIII	IIII	IIII
1967	IIII	III	IIII	III
1968	III	III	III	III
1969	III	II	III	II
1970	II	II	II	II
1971	II	I	II	I
1972	I	I	I	I
1973	I		I	
1974	////	////	////	////
1975	////	///	////	///
1976	///	///	///	///
1977	///	//	///	//
1978	//	//	//	//
1979	/	//	//	/

*For description of dating code on WWII black crackle lighter, see page 6.

ZIPPO LIGHTER IDENTIFICATION CODES

YEAR	REGULAR		SLIM	
	LEFT	RIGHT	LEFT	RIGHT
1980	/	/	/	/
1981		/		
1982	\\\\	\\\\	\\\\	\\\\
1983	\\\\	\\\	\\\\	\\\
1984	\\\	\\\	\\\	\\\
1985	\\\	\\	\\	\\
1986	\\	\\	\\	\\

EFFECTIVE 7-1-86 THE ABOVE SYSTEM WAS REPLACED BY YEAR/LOT CODE. YEAR IS NOTED WITH ROMAN NUMERAL/ LETTER DESIGNATES LOT MONTH (A=JAN., B=FEB. etc.)

YEAR	REGULAR		SLIM	
1986	A to L	II	SAME AS REGULAR	
1987	A to L	III	SAME AS REGULAR	
1988	A to L	IV	SAME AS REGULAR	
1989	A to L	V	SAME AS REGULAR	
1990	A to L	VI	SAME AS REGULAR	
1991	A to L	VII	SAME AS REGULAR	
1992	A to L	VIII	SAME AS REGULAR	
1993	A to L	IX	SAME AS REGULAR	
1994	A to L	X	SAME AS REGULAR	
1995	A to L	XI	SAME AS REGULAR	
1996	A to L	XII	SAME AS REGULAR	
1997	A to L	XIII	SAME AS REGULAR	
1998	A to L	XIV	SAME AS REGULAR	
1999	A to L	XV	SAME AS REGULAR	
2000	A to L	XVI	SAME AS REGULAR	

ZIPPO, 1930s. A group of 1930s Zippos. Notice that the outside hinges have been replaced. The original outside hinges would have had a chrome finish. These have a nickel finish. The lighter on the right is a 1936 square model and was also repaired. It originally had a 4 barrel hinge but now has a 3 barrel hinge. In the second photo, you can see that the first, second, and fourth lighters are 1934 models and the third lighter is an inside hinge 1936 model. Values with the repairs are $400-$700 for the 1934 models and $150-250 for the 1936 model.

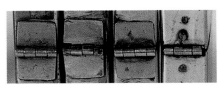

ZIPPO, c.1932. Zippo's first model. This particular model was never chrome plated. It stood 5/16 of an inch taller than the later Zippos. They were bigger because the insert was bigger. Some people feel that the first model was actually produced in 1933. Value: $3,000-5,000.

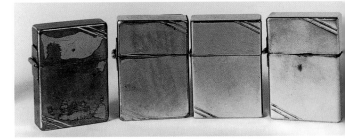

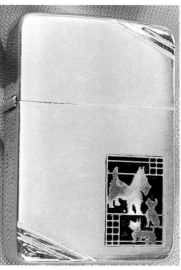

ZIPPO, 1937. An unusual Scottie dog design on an early Zippo. The lighter has a 4 barrel hinge and a brushed chrome finish. The Scottie dog design is a "Metalique" applied by Zippo. Value: $750-1,000.

ZIPPO, c.1938. An early Zippo lighter in its original "Windy" box. Value: $500-800 (lighter w/ original box).

ZIPPO, 1938- 1941. This was the first model Zippo "Barcroft" table model lighter. It has an unusual 4 barrel hinge with a large insert and a single stepped base. 5" tall. Value: $800-1,000.

ZIPPO, c.1938. Early Zippo lighter "Windy" boxes. The box can be found in two color variations: silver & black and gold & black. Value: $150-175 (w/ original box).

ZIPPO, 1940s. Early Zippo lighter boxes. The box on the right is harder to find. Value: (L-R) $50, $95.

ZIPPO, 1943. A war time steel lighter with the owner's name, location, and date engraved upon it. Paul Foyres, Sicily, 1943. Value: $75-125.

ZIPPO, Mid-1940s. Zippo lighter boxes available during the War that would have held the black crackle finish lighters. Value: $250-450 (w/ lighter).

ZIPPO, c.1948. An early 3 barrel hinge Sports lighter with a golfer and engraved with his country club's initials. Value: $100-175.

ZIPPO, c.1946. A group of 1940s Zippo lighters as mementoes of different places or events. While most Zippo lighters were chrome plating over brass, these 3 barrel hinge lighters were made of nickel silver. Value: $100-150 ea. (if all original).

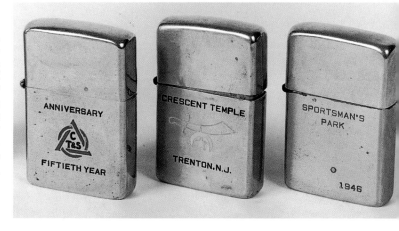

ZIPPO, 1950/51. A lighter with a brown leather wrap. This has a 2032695 patent with a 5 barrel hinge. Value: $250-350.

ZIPPO, c.1950. A fantastic GE TV with Ultra-Vision advertiser. Unusual because the body is lacquered front and back and decorated to look like a 1950 television console. Value: $300-400.

ZIPPO, c.1950. Two very rare Zippos that used to belong to employees. Some employees would take the old design room lighters that the company no longer needed. Some of the familiar designs were the Reveler, also called the Drunk On A Lamppost, and the elephant from the early Sports series. Value: $200-800, depending on the images.

ZIPPO, early 1950s. Zippo slim lighter boxes. The box on the right is hinged with two pins and is difficult to find. Value: (L-R) $20 (box only), $65.

ZIPPO, 1950s. Zippo lighter blue and white striped box. Value: $20-30.

ZIPPO, c. 1952. A rectangular Zippo gift box that includes a lighter, flints, and fluid.

ZIPPO, 1950s. A gift box that includes flint, fuel, and lighter.

ZIPPO, c.1952. Here is an example of a great Zippo. Desi Arnez and Lucille Ball were America's sweethearts that appeared on Television in TV's early days. Assigning a value is difficult, but this lighter sold for $1,200 at auction. Value: $1,000-1,200.

ZIPPO, 1952. A Zippo advertiser with Happy Hotpoint. Happy was the Hotpoint Appliance company's cartoon figure for many years. Value: $60-90.

ZIPPO, 1950s. A group of Sterling silver models from the 1950s. Value: $100-225.

ZIPPO-TIFFANY, 1953. A rare slim size lighter made of Sterling silver, marked "Tiffany & Co." and sporting an Indian Head penny. Value: $150-300.

ZIPPO, c.1953. A wonderful Zippo that belonged to a fellow named Rene. Sterling silver in a hard green box. Value: $125-200.

ZIPPO, c.1955 &1965. Zippo lighter boxes. The striped box on the right is the earlier of the two. Value: (L-R) $25, $35 (including a standard lighter).

ZIPPO, 1957. A 50th anniversary advertiser for Spring City Knitting with a unique custom printed box. Value: $150-250.

ZIPPO, c.1957. A pair of lighters advertising Esso Gasoline. Value: $75-125.

ZIPPO, c.1958. A wonderful advertiser for the Sports News out of Chicago, Illinois. Three sporting images on one lighter. Value: $40-70.

ZIPPO, c.1958. The Zippo "Gift Set" included the lighter, flints, and fuel. Value: $150-225.

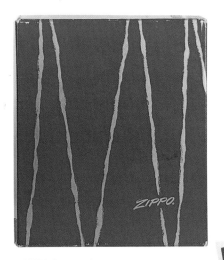

ZIPPO, c. 1959. A green Zippo gift box that includes a lighter, flints, and fluid.

ZIPPO, c.1960. The Zippo "Gift Set" included the lighter, flints, and fuel. Value: $150-225.

ZIPPO, 1960. A nice Zippo advertising piece—a penny on a chain. Value: $20-30.

ZUNDER, c.1943. German made Augusta-Zunder wick lighters with an abalone covering and gold plated metal. The mechanism works when the lighter is lifted. 4" tall. Value: $35-55.

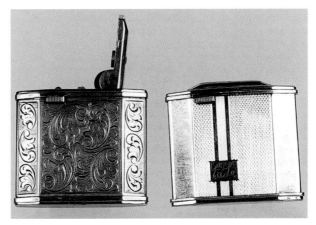

ZUNDER, c.1954. A pair of Zunder lighters. When the button is pulled back, the top opens and the lighter lights. Engraved Sterling silver on the left and silver plated on the right. 2.5" tall. Value: $30-80.

ZUNDER, c.1950. A leather covered gold plated lighter. When the wheel is turned, the top opens and the lighter lights. 2.5" tall. Value: $30-40.

ZUNDER, c.1964. A 14kt gold jacketed gas automatic lighter. This is a very elegant lighter. 2.5" tall. Value: $175-250.

CLEANING LIGHTERS

Almost all lighters will look substantially better with a thorough cleaning. The main component of grime is built-up oily carbon. Start cleaning with a cotton swab and a sharpened popsicle stick. The wood will scrape off the carbon and not scratch the metal. With a little work, most of the carbon will come off. The cotton swab will remove the loosened grime. You can dip it in lighter fluid to float the grime off. Clean out the grooves of the friction wheel with a scalpel or Exacto knife. Outside metal parts can be buffed on a buffing wheel. I use a plastic polish that is available in most hardware stores. Use one wheel on metal and a separate wheel on plastic or painted areas. Go lightly as the buffing compound can cut through paint or a thin plating and reach the base metal.

Old flints tend to disintegrate or attach themselves to the sides of the flint tube. A drill bit of the proper size will help to remove the frozen flint. Try turning it by hand to start, and if you have no success, then use it in the drill. Be warned that some of the flint tubes are curved and a drill may destroy the curved tube. Work slowly. If you see any brass colored bits coming out when you drill, stop immediately. A piece of coat hanger will sometimes work to push out a frozen flint. Once the flint tube is cleared, it also works well to scrape out the bits of frozen flint remaining. If you are not going to use the lighter, do not put a new flint in.

If the wick is gone or too frayed, then you may need to install a new wick. Zippo makes and sells replacement wicks that will work. Or an alternative is to take a wick from a lighter in your parts box. You may have to remove the felt stuffing of the lighter to get the wick into place. It should be long enough to reach from the spark area to the felt stuffing that holds the lighter fluid.

RESOURCES

Vintage Lighters, Inc., P.O. Box 1325, Fair Lawn, New Jersey 07410. Contact Ira Pilossof at 201-797-6595, email him at **Vintageltr@aol.com**. Dealer in vintage lighters.

Authorized Repair Service, 30 W. 57th Street, New York, New York 10019. Does lighter repair.

International Lighter Collectors Club, P.O. Box 1733, Quitman, Texas 75783. The largest lighter club. Publishes "OTLS," *On The Lighter Side* newsletter. Has information on the lighter shows.

Pocket Lighter Preservation Guild, c/o Karen Cairo, P.O. Box 1054, Addison, IL 60101. Lighter club.

eBay—The Online Auction place. It is located at www.ebay.com

BIBLIOGRAPHY

Balfour, Michael. *Alfred Dunhill: 100 Years & More*. London, England: Weidenfeld & Nicolson, 1994.

Bisconcini, Stephano. *Lighters/Accendini*. Milano, Italy: Edizioni San Gottardo, 1983.

Clayton, Larry. *The Evans Book*. Atglen, PA: Schiffer Publishing Ltd., 1998.

Cummings, U.K. *Ronson—The World's Greatest Lighter*. Palo Alto, CA: Bird Dog Books, 1992.

Schneider, Stuart, & George Fischler. *Cigarette Lighters*. Atglen, PA: Schiffer Publishing Ltd., 1996.

Van Weert, Ad, & Joop Bromet. *The Legend of the Lighter*. New York, New York: Abbeville Press, 1995.